Charles Quennell

The cathedral church of Norwich

A description of its fabric and a brief history of the episcopal see

Charles Quennell

The cathedral church of Norwich
A description of its fabric and a brief history of the episcopal see

ISBN/EAN: 9783337259518

Printed in Europe, USA, Canada, Australia, Japan

Cover: Foto ©Lupo / pixelio.de

More available books at **www.hansebooks.com**

THE CATHEDRAL CHURCH OF NORWICH

A DESCRIPTION OF ITS FABRIC AND A BRIEF HISTORY OF THE EPISCOPAL SEE

BY

C. H. B. QUENNELL

WITH FORTY 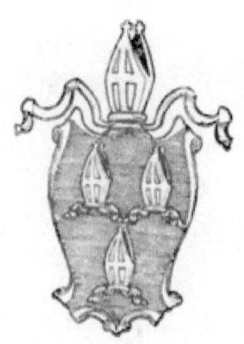 ILLUSTRATIONS

LONDON   GEORGE BELL & SONS   1898

W. H. WHITE AND CO. LIMITED
RIVERSIDE PRESS, EDINBURGH

GENERAL PREFACE

THIS series of monographs has been planned to supply visitors to the great English Cathedrals with accurate and well illustrated guide-books at a popular price. The aim of each writer has been to produce a work compiled with sufficient knowledge and scholarship to be of value to the student of Archæology and History, and yet not too technical in language for the use of an ordinary visitor or tourist.

To specify all the authorities which have been made use of in each case would be difficult and tedious in this place. But amongst the general sources of information which have been almost invariably found useful are:—(1) the great county histories, the value of which, especially in questions of genealogy and local records, is generally recognised; (2) the numerous papers by experts which appear from time to time in the Transactions of the Antiquarian and Archæological Societies; (3) the important documents made accessible in the series issued by the Master of the Rolls; (4) the well-known works of Britton and Willis on the English Cathedrals; and (5) the very excellent series of Handbooks to the Cathedrals originated by the late Mr John Murray; to which the reader may in most cases be referred for fuller detail, especially in reference to the histories of the respective sees.

GLEESON WHITE,
EDWARD F. STRANGE,
Editors of the Series.

AUTHOR'S PREFACE

THE task of writing a monograph, on such an essentially Norman Cathedral as Norwich, has been most pleasing to one who owns to an especial fondness for that sturdy architecture which was evolved in England during one of her stormiest epochs—from the end of the eleventh till the end of the twelfth century.

I would here acknowledge indebtedness and thanks due to the Very Rev. the Dean and Mrs Sheepshanks for the personal interest they evinced, and for his material help; to Mr J. B. Spencer, the sub-sacrist, for that help which his intimate association with the cathedral enabled him to offer; and to Mr S. K. Greenslade for the loan of the drawings reproduced under his name; as well as to the Photochrom Co. Ltd., Messrs S. B. Bolas & Co., and Mr F. G. M. Beaumont for the use of their photographs. The views of the cathedral as it appeared in the early part of the nineteenth century are reproduced from Britton's "Norwich," and from a volume by Charles Wild.

C. H. B. Q.

CONTENTS

	PAGE
CHAPTER I.—History of the Fabric	3
CHAPTER II.—The Cathedral—Exterior	23
The Cathedral Precincts	23
The Erpingham Gate	23
St. Ethelbert's Gate and the Gate-House	25
Chapel of St. John the Evangelist	27
The West Front of the Cathedral	28
Exterior of Nave	31
The South Transept	32
The Diocesan Registry Offices and Slype	35
The Chapter-House	36
The Tower and Spire	36
The Eastern Arm of Cathedral or Presbytery	39
The Chapels of St. Mary-the-Less and Saint Luke	39, 40
The Jesus Chapel and Reliquary Chapel	40
The North Transept	40
The Bishop's Palace	43
CHAPTER III.—The Interior	45
The Nave	45
The Choir Screen	49
The Nave Vault	50
The West Window and West Door	55
The North and South Aisles of Nave	55, 56
Monuments in Nave and Aisles of Nave	57, 58
The Cloisters	58
The Walks—East, South, and West	62, 63
The Ante-choir and Choir	64
The Pelican Lectern	68
The Presbytery	68
Reliquary Chapel	72
Monuments in the Presbytery	74
The North Transept	76
The Tower and Triforium Walks	79
The Processional Path	79
The Jesus Chapel	83
St. Luke's Chapel	88
Treasury and Muniment Room	88
The Bauchon Chapel	88
The South Transept	88
Monuments	91
CHAPTER IV.—The Sees of the East Anglian Bishops	95
CHAPTER V.—The City	111

LIST OF ILLUSTRATIONS

	PAGE
Norwich Cathedral from the South-East . . *Frontispiece*	
Arms of Norwich . . . . *Title*	
The Cathedral from the South-West	2
The Cathedral in the Seventeenth Century	9
West Front of the Cathedral in 1816	15
The Cathedral from the South-West Angle of Cloisters . .	22
The Erpingham Gate	24
St. Ethelbert's Gate	26
The Gate-House of the Bishop's Palace	27
West Front of the Cathedral	29
The Clerestory and Triforium of Choir (South Side) . .	33
The Tower in 1816	37
Exterior of the Chapel of St. Luke from the East . .	41
A Norman Capital	46
The Nave, looking East	47
The Choir Screen and Organ from the Nave . . .	51
The North Aisle of Nave, looking West	56
The East Walk of the Cloisters	58
The Cloisters from the Garth	59
The Prior's Door	63
The Choir and Presbytery	65
A Stall in the Choir	67
The Choir and Presbytery in 1816	69
The Choir Stalls at the beginning of the Nineteenth Century .	71
The Choir, looking West	73
Detail of the Presbytery Clerestory and Vaulting . . .	75
The Choir Apse	77
Detail of the Clerestory, North Transept	80
The South Aisle of Presbytery, looking East . . .	81
Norman Work in the Lantern of Tower	83
The Ante-Reliquary Bridge Chapel	84
Doorway and Screen between South Transept and Aisle of Presbytery	85
View across the Apse from the Chapel of St. Luke . .	89
The Resurrection: from the Painted Retable formerly in the Jesus Chapel	93
Norwich Castle	99
The Guildhall	103
Monument of Bishop Goldwell	107
The Pelican Lectern in the Choir	110
Pull's Ferry	112
PLAN OF THE CATHEDRAL	113

A

Photochrom Co. Ltd., Photo.] THE CATHEDRAL FROM THE SOUTH-WEST.

NORWICH CATHEDRAL

CHAPTER I

HISTORY OF THE FABRIC OF THE CATHEDRAL CHURCH OF
THE HOLY TRINITY OF NORWICH

NORWICH CATHEDRAL stands on the site of no earlier church: it is to-day, in its plan and the general bulk of its detail, as characteristically Norman as when left finished by the hand of Eborard, the second bishop of Norwich.

The church was founded by Herbert de Losinga, the first bishop, as the cathedral priory of the Benedictine monastery in Norwich (a sketch of its constitution at this period will be found in the Notes on the Diocese); the foundation-stone was laid in 1096 on a piece of land called Cowholme,—meaning a pasture surrounded by water,—and the church was dedicated to the Holy Trinity.

It may be of interest to the tourist and student to review briefly what sort and manner of man Herbert the founder was; what had been his environment prior to his appointment as the first bishop of Norwich; and what the causes were which had as their effect the building of the cathedral.

The characteristics of the cathedral are — its long nave, which is typical of the Norman church; its glorious apsidal termination, encircled by a procession path, which recalls the plan of a French cathedral; and the form of this, with the remains of its old bishops' chair centrally placed, and with the westward position, of the throne at Torcello and other Italian churches, of the basilican type of plan.

Herbert, surnamed de Losinga, transferred the see from Thetford to Norwich in 1094, and it is from this period that the history of the cathedral may be said to commence.

Herbert was a prelate of a type that in the early days helped to build up the Church and give her stability. His nature must have been curiously complex; on the one hand, a man of action and with great capability of administration, often justifying his means by the end he had in view, and not being debarred from realising his schemes by any delicate scruples, he yet, on the other hand, presents in his letters a chastened spirituality that is not compatible with the methods he pursued when thinking only of the temporal advantages which might accrue on any certain line of action. But it may be said that his letters appear to date from the later period of his life, and after he had founded the cathedral as an expiation of that sin of simony he appears to have so deeply repented.

Yet in the earlier period, which we shall note, he was emphatically the man of action, the typical administrator, who, mixing freely in the political life of the times, was strengthening the position of the Church, and gradually leading her up to that position, which she ultimately gained, of Arbitress of Kings and Empires.

He had also a morbid belief in the power of money—he probably would have agreed that "every man has his price," and his simoniacal dealings with William Rufus, which procured his preferment to Norwich, afford evidence of this weak trait in his character.

Herbert's birthplace is disputed, and, as Dean Goulburn remarked, this is but natural: a man so justly celebrated would not, or, rather, historians will not be content with one; so that though he cannot rival Homer in that seven cities desired to be accredited each as his birthplace, yet Herbert falls not far short, and this fact alone will perhaps give some idea of his popularity during his life, and the interest then aroused which has lasted down to our own times. From a small pamphlet issued by the dean and chapter in 1896, and containing extracts from the *Registrum Primum*, we learn that "In primis Ecclesiam prefatam fundavit piæ memoriæ Herbertus Episcopus, qui Normanniæ in pago Oximensi natus." First Herbert, the bishop, of pious memory, who was born in Normandy, in the district of Oximin (or Exmes).

This seems very credible, and the old monkish chronicler who was responsible for the *Registrum Primum* and its rugged Latin, may have had authentic proof of the truth of his assertion. The manuscript dates from the thirteenth century, and no considerable period, historically considered, had then passed since Herbert had been one of the prime movers of the religious and political life of the day.

Blomefield, the antiquary, attributed to him a Suffolk extraction, and then again spoke of his Norman descent: thus agreeing in some measure with the *Registrum Primum*. And again, another idea is that he was born in the hundred of Hoxne, where he possessed property, and his father before him.

Herbert had, we know, received his education in Normandy, and had taken his vows at, and ultimately had risen to be prior of, the Abbey of Fécamp in Normandy; and it was while vigorously administering this office that he received an invitation from William Rufus to come to England, being offered as an inducement the appointment of Abbot of Ramsey.

And no doubt from this period the spiritual side of his duties must of necessity have been somewhat neglected. From the position of prior of Fécamp, his circle of power limited to the neighbourhood of his priory, and his duties rounded by the due observance of the rules of his order, he was given at once the administration of what was one of the richest abbeys in England, and attained at once the power of a great feudal lord. He was Sewer to William Rufus as well, an office endowed with fees and perquisites, and so to Herbert came the temptation of accumulating wealth for his own ambitious ends. It was not, however, the sin of a small man: he introduced no personal element into his greed, but rather thought of his party and his Church, although, of necessity, an environment so purely temporal told on the spiritual side of his character. It might be best to connect the links of the East Anglian bishoprics here, although in the notes on the diocese the matter is gone into at more length.

Herbert de Losinga was the first bishop of Norwich, to which town the see was transferred in compliance with a decree of Lanfranc's Synod, held in 1075, that all sees should be fixed at the principal towns in their dioceses.

Felix was the first bishop of East Anglia, and fixed his see at Dunwich in 630.

The see was divided by Theodore, Archbishop of Canterbury, in 669 into those of Elmham and Dunwich; and these again were united under Wildred in 870, and the see fixed at

Elmham, and where it remained till 1070, when Herfast, a chaplain of William the Conqueror's, moved his see to Thetford.

Now, about this time, when Herbert was abbot of Ramsey and Sewer to William Rufus, the see of Thetford was vacant, and Herbert gave the king to understand that if he was appointed to the vacant bishopric, and his father made Abbot of Winchester, he was willing and able to pay for such preferment a sum of £1900: a part of his accumulated savings, no doubt, and a very large amount for that time.

William II. made these appointments, and the sum mentioned was paid into the royal treasury; but the bishop found that he had attained his end at a cost other than he had reckoned on; public opinion in those days was quite as powerful a force as it is now, though the channels along which its force could be felt and its strength find expression were limited. Indignation was rife, and monkish versifiers and chroniclers protested in lines more or less uncomplimentary, and more or less forcible, their loathing of such sin of simony.

Now it is probable that, in expiation of this transgression, Herbert came to build Norwich Cathedral. It is certain that he almost at once repented. In after years, in his letters, he says, "I entered on mine office disgracefully, but by the help of God's grace I shall pass out of it with credit."

In Dean Goulburn's admirable monograph on the cathedral many of Herbert's letters are given, and these alone would go to stamp him as a wonderful man. His conscience was awakened by the popular outcry against his sin of simony, he plunged into his new duties at Thetford with ardour in the vain hope of distraction, but failed to find that consolation he had hoped to; and so about 1093 he determined on a visit to Rome to tender his resignation and confess his sin to Pope Urban. He journeyed to Rome and was kindly received, and the absolution he desired readily granted. The Pope was glad to see an English bishop come to him for advice, and in granting him absolution he strengthened considerably his claim to be regarded as head of the English Church.

This lengthy preamble may seem somewhat unjustifiable, but if we are to study any building aright, and if we are to interpret in any measure its meaning and symbolism, it cannot wholly be done on any line of abstract æstheticism or arch-

HISTORY OF THE FABRIC

æological instinct, however intuitive it may be: we must in some measure think of the builders of old times and of the influences which with them produced its inception and have left it to come down the ages to us.

It is interesting to note that Herbert's early French training influenced him in the planning of the beautiful eastern termination to his cathedral, and the grand sweep of the procession path. Similar apsidal terminations, of slightly later date, once existed at Ely, and still remain in a modified form at Peterborough.

The old tribunal arrangement of presbyters' seats with the central bishop's throne facing west, which was part of Herbert's first plan, no doubt may safely be accredited to the influence of his journey to Rome, and where he may have become familar with what was the usual basilican arrangement.

Herbert returned to England, penitent and forgiven for his sin, and it is probable that the Pope had laid on him, as a penance, an injunction to build churches and found religious houses, and that with the remainder of his wealth he determined to transfer the see from Thetford to Norwich and to build in the latter place his cathedral church. It would also have been in compliance with the decree of Lanfranc's Synod. The see was transferred on the 9th of April 1094, and Herbert was consecrated on the same day by Thomas, Archbishop of York.

Norwich was then an important town; in the Middle Ages it ranked as the second city in the kingdom. Its prosperity was chiefly due to its large trade in wool. It is a moot point whether the town was ever a settlement of the Romans, no traces of such occupation having ever been discovered. The castle mound, no doubt, formed some part of the earthworks of an earlier stronghold. The word Norwich is probably of Norse origin, meaning the north village or the village on the North Creek ("*wic*"—*i.e.* a creek). The city stood on a tidal bay in 1004, in which year the Danes under Sweyn completely devastated and ruined the town in revenge for the massacre of their countrymen by Æthelred the Unready two years before. So that the history of the town of Norwich, as we now know it, may be said to have started directly after this.

The foundation-stone of the cathedral was laid in 1096;

and upon it, according to the *Registrum Primum*, the following inscription is said to have been placed:—" In nomine patris et filii et spiritus Sancti Amen Ego Herbertus Episcopus apposui istum lapidem." (In the Name of the Father and of the Son and of the Holy Ghost, Amen, I, Herbert the Bishop, have placed this stone.)

It was the custom of the Norman builders to start building from the easternmost part of the church, as the more sacred part of the structure, and then build westwards; so that probably this foundation-stone, for which diligent search has been made in vain, was in the eastmost wall of the original Norman Lady Chapel—in fact, the *Registrum Primum* describes how Herbert began the work "where is now the chapel of the Blessed Mary." This chapel was demolished to make way for the beautiful thirteenth-century Lady Chapel which Dean Gardiner destroyed.

The thirteenth-century builders of the Lady Chapel may have used Herbert's foundation-stone in their walling; Dean Lefroy quite lately, while repairing parts of the tower and east end, came across pieces of stone with beautiful "dog-tooth" ornament upon them, which had been used to repair the masonry that, it was evident, at one time had formed part of the thirteenth-century Lady Chapel. This must be so, since in no other part of the building save the arches now remaining in the extreme eastern wall of the procession path, which at one time gave access to the Lady Chapel, does such ornament occur.

It is probable, and the more generally accredited supposition, that Herbert built the presbytery with its encircling procession path and the original trefoil of Norman chapel radiating therefrom;—the choir and transepts with the two chapels projecting eastwards and the first two bays of the nave. Harrod advances a theory that he completely finished the whole of the cathedral church, as well as the offices for the housing of the sixty monks who were placed therein, in 1101.

He also built the episcopal palace on the north side of the cathedral, of which some parts remain to this day incorporated with work of a later period; he seems to have founded and built other churches in Norwich and Yarmouth. He died on the 22nd of July 1119, in the twenty-ninth year of

THE CATHEDRAL IN THE SEVENTEENTH CENTURY.

his episcopate, and was buried before the high altar in his own cathedral church.

Bishop Eborard, who succeeded in 1121, is credited with having finished the nave from the point where Herbert had left it. The evidence which goes to support this theory is taken from the *Registrum Primum*. "Moreover, the same Herbert completed the church of Norwich in his own time, as I have learned from the account of old people, but have not found in writing, as far as the altar of the Holy Cross, which is now called the altar of St. William. He also built all the episcopal dwelling-house, except the great hall." The altar referred to was on the north side of choir screen.

Herbert also provided the base for the tower only, probably up to the roof level; the remainder, up to the parapet, was finished about the time of Henry I., but at that earlier period it was without the stone spire which now adds dignity to the cathedral from any point of view.

The roofs at this time were generally of a flat wooden construction throughout (similar to that of Peterborough Cathedral), and probably decorated with lozenges, flowers, and symbolical devices. When recently, under Dean Lefroy, the whitewash and paint were cleaned off from the stonework, many indications have been found of a most beautiful scheme of colour decoration.

Though we, in this part, are following up the history of the cathedral structure, yet it may be interesting to note that it was during the episcopate of Bishop Eborard that the boy saint, St. William of Norwich, was said to have been martyred. He was the son of country folk who gained a living by agriculture. During his life he worked many miracles, and by his death gave Norwich a share of his glory. It is related that he was tortured by the Jews, and on the spot where they were discovered secretly burying him, in Thorpe Wood, a chapel was erected called the Chapel of St. William in the Wood. Very little now remains of this structure, but the site can still be traced. The altar before referred to was set up to his memory in Norwich Cathedral, on the north side of the screen leading into the ante-choir.

Bishop Eborard resigned the see, or was deposed in 1145, and retired to the abbey of Fontenay, Mont-Bard, Côte d'Or, in the South of France. He had re-enforced a mandate of Herbert's that the clergy of the diocese should contribute to the fund in aid of the fabric.

During the episcopate of Eborard's successor, Bishop William de Turbe, the cathedral appears neither to have gained or suffered until, about 1169 or 1170, a fire broke out in the monastic buildings; the fire-extinguishing appliances in those days, if indeed there were any at all, could not prevent it spreading to the cathedral. It is generally believed that the original Norman Lady Chapel was also well destroyed.

Bishop William de Turbe, although an old man at the time (he died in 1174), is said to have taken a vow that he would not go from within twelve leucas of the cathedral, unless compelled by the direst necessity, until the ravages of the flames had been repaired. He is reported to have seated himself at the door of the cathedral, and to have begged alms for this purpose from the worshippers. The work of reparation was carried on by his successor, John of Oxford, who may also be said to have completely finished Herbert's cathedral. He provided the furniture of the church, the vestments, books and ornaments, and, probably, entirely re-modelled the monastic buildings. He is also said to have built the Infirmary, of which now only three piers remain, to the south of the cloisters.

In the years following, various works were doubtless carried on, but it is not until the time of Walter de Suffield, about 1250, that anything important in the way of structural alteration was effected. The fire of 1169 had in part or whole destroyed the original Norman Lady Chapel, and Bishop de Turbe had restored the same in some measure. But the *cultus* of the Blessed Virgin in the interval had gathered strength wonderfully; chapels dedicated to her naturally became important, and Bishop Suffield determined to pull down the old Norman work and rebuild a chapel in the Early English style then prevalent. Dean Goulburn, in his work on the cathedral, estimated the size of the later chapel at 90 feet long by 30 feet wide, and these dimensions are shown plotted in dotted lines on the plan in this book. This is longer and narrower than the size given in previous conjectures, but Dean Goulburn had the opportunity of inspecting the foundations of the chapel, which, with those of the still earlier one, lie buried but a few feet below the surface in a garden to the east of the

HISTORY OF THE FABRIC

cathedral. In the same place, and over the entrance arches remaining, the height and lines of the later roof can be seen still plainly marked on the stonework. These entrance arches are beautifully moulded and decorated on the inside with the "dog-tooth" ornament—a decoration peculiar to the Early English style.

The theological reaction which followed close on this movement led to the neglect of the chapel, and obviated the necessity of maintaining it as a place of worship. It had probably greatly decayed; that Dean Gardiner (1573-89), no longer needing it for services, was tempted to pull it down, as a cheaper expedient than keeping it in repair.

In 1271 Norwich was visited by a terrific thunderstorm, when the tower was struck by lightning. The damage, however, was not great, as, fortunately, the excessive rains which followed quenched the fire that had been kindled. This incident, however, was the precursor of one of the stormiest periods in the history of the city and its cathedral church. Roger de Skerning occupied the episcopal chair, and the prior was one William de Brunham, a man of fierce and truculent disposition. An outbreak of hostilities between the citizens on the one hand and the monks on the other, was brought about by his arbitrary assumption of power; the bishop throughout, ostensibly preferring the safer game of a somewhat anomalous position of neutrality, is nevertheless believed to have covertly sanctioned his proceedings.

A fair was held in Tombland—to the west of the precincts—annually on Trinity Sunday, and by right of ancient custom the priors reaped large revenues by the imposition of tolls on the sales. Tombland, derived from *Tomeland*, a vacant space, had originally formed part of the estate bequeathed by Herbert, the founder, to the monks; the boundaries in course of time had become matters of controversy, and it is probable that the citizens felt the imposition of these tolls and dues to be a real and serious grievance. A riot broke out and the monks were driven within their gates. Had the prior at this juncture chosen to act peacefully, it is probable that history would contain no record of the sacrilege that followed. He, however, decided to resist force by force, and carefully generaled his monks, disposing them at the various strategetic points of his domain. At the same time he sent to Yarmouth for mercenaries—these arrived and the tables were turned; the prior's forces sallied forth from the gates and robbed and pillaged the town.

The citizens, roused to a pitch of madness, drove them and the soldiers back again within the walls of the monastery; the bishop, instead of acting as peacemaker, appears to have preserved his position of neutrality and quietly stopped in his palace. There was a short interval of truce, but it only served as a breath to fan the flames; the citizens besieged the cathedral precincts, and by the means probably of slings succeeded in hurling combustible materials into the buildings, with a result that the whole of the monastery and the cathedral itself was soon in flames. It seems to be an established fact that the prior had placed men in the tower to shoot at the citizens, and it is conjectured that they, and not the citizens, were the cause of the outbreak here.

The only part of the cathedral that escaped was the Lady Chapel; the rest was gutted, vestments and ornaments were carried off, and the monks for the most part slain.

So ended the first part of this lamentable chapter in the history of Norwich. A sentence of excommunication was passed on the city, and King Henry hastened to Norwich to preside at the trial of the prisoners.

The accounts which have come down to us are as varied as might be expected, the chroniclers of the one party, of course, blaming the other side; it seems, however, to have been proved "that, after all, the church was burnt by that accursed prior"; but many of the citizens were hung, drawn and quartered, and the city had to pay in all 3000 marks towards repairing the church and monastical buildings, and to provide a gold pyx, weighing ten pounds, of gold; the monks in their turn had to make new gates and entrances into the precincts. The St. Ethelbert's Gate-house was part of the work imposed on the monks; it is of early Decorated character and was erected probably early in the fourteenth century.

Bishop Roger de Skerning had died in retirement on the 22nd of January 1277, and in the meantime the work of reparation had proceeded with such vigour that on Advent Sunday 1278 his successor, Bishop Middleton, was inaugurated with great state; Edward I. and his Queen with the Bishops

THE WEST FRONT OF THE CATHEDRAL IN 1816.

of London, Hereford, and Waterford being present. He does not seem to have done much in the way of building, though the work of reparation was carried on; he died in 1287, and it was left to his successor, Bishop Ralph de Walpole, to begin the work of rebuilding the cloisters. The original Norman cloisters, which had endured until the time of the great fire in 1272, were probably of wood. It was determined to rebuild them in stone in the prevailing style. The cloisters are described in more detail in the notes on the interior of the cathedral, so that it will be sufficient to state here that their building spread over a period of one hundred and thirty-three years, and that they were finished during the episcopate of Bishop Alnwick.

Bishop Walpole built the eastern walk of the cloisters, together with the chapter-house; he was translated to Ely about 1299, and the work carried on by his successor, Bishop Salmon, who built the south walk, also a chapel and hall attached to the bishop's palace. Of this nothing remains in the garden of the palace except a grand ruin, which is supposed to have formed the entrance or porch to the hall.

He founded also the chapel dedicated to St. John the Evangelist, converted by Edward VI. into, and now used as, a grammar school; below it was a charnel-house.

Continuing the history of the fabric, we can pass on to the episcopate of Bishop Percy, during which, about 1361, the wooden spire and parts of central tower of the cathedral were blown down by a violent gale of wind, and the presbytery was greatly damaged by the falling material. This bishop rebuilt the present clerestory, designed in the transitional style between Decorated and Perpendicular; the vault is later. It is also probable that he repaired the spire.

During Bishop Wakering's time the Erpingham gate of the close was erected, and as well the cloister that formerly connected the palace on the north side with the cathedral. He also founded a chantry for one monk at his tomb.

His successor, Alnwick, completed the cloisters. The gateway to the palace was built by him about 1430, and probably replaced an earlier structure. He also began the work of remodelling the central compartment of the west front. He left directions in his will to his executors to make a large west window, the cost to be charged to his estate. The doorway under this window, built over the old Norman one, and encroaching on the side arcading, was executed during his episcopate, the window being eventually added during the time of Bishop Lyhart to throw additional light on to the vault he erected, and its wonderful sculptures.

In 1446, on February 27th, Walter Lyhart, or le Hart, was consecrated, and it is to him that Norwich Cathedral owes the superb *lierne* vault that now spans the nave. Other important works were carried out by him; the spire which had been blown down in 1362 (and had probably been re-constructed by Bishop Percy—though there is no record of such work), was struck by lightning in 1463, and the burning mass fell through the presbytery roof, which up till this period was still in wood, completely destroying it, and making necessary the vault added by Lyhart's successor.

During this episcopate the rood screen was erected, and a sumptuous monument placed over the grave of the founder.

The stone spire must have been added about this time, replacing the former wooden construction.

Bishop Lyhart left to his successor, Bishop Goldwell, in his will 2200 marks for repairing the dilapidations caused by the fire of 1463. During this bishop's episcopate we find that the cathedral was brought nearly to that state in which we have it now,—the tower was still further adorned with Perpendicular battlements, the presbytery was vaulted in with stone, and the flying-buttresses added around the eastern apse to take the consequent thrust of the new vault.

Internally, also, the lower stages of the presbytery were Perpendicularised by the addition of the four centred arches that still remain, and in the second bay of which, eastward from the tower, on the south side, was erected Bishop Goldwell's altar tomb.

His successor, Lane, occupied the see but a short while, 1499-1500, and in turn was succeeded by Bishop Nykke—he is more generally called *Nix* (snow), sarcastically, as his character appears to have been of the blackest. During his episcopate, the cathedral was again visited by fire in 1509. The sacristy, with all the books and ornaments, was consumed, and the wooden roofs of both transepts totally destroyed.

Bishop Nykke constructed the stone vaulting that, covering both arms of the church, completed the stone vaulting throughout the cathedral. His chantry, which is on the south side of the nave, and occupies two bays of the aisle, was arranged by him before his death, and its richness is inversely proportionate to the degradation of his character.

The tracery in the Norman arch leading from the south aisle of the presbytery into the transept, is of late Perpendicular style, and was added by Robert of Calton, who was destined to be the last prior but one of Norwich: William Castleton was the last prior and the first dean. Bishop Nykke died in 1535-6, and was succeeded by William Rupgg or Repes, who was the last bishop elected by the chapter of the monks of the Benedictine monastery of Norwich. Monasticism was doomed; Wolsey had fallen, and his property had been confiscated in 1529. The smaller monasteries were dissolved in 1536, and in 1538 the greater shared the same fate, among them Norwich.

Most interesting is the parallel which can be drawn between the history of the Church and of that architecture which she especially fostered. Gothic or Christian art was developed from the remains of a Roman civilisation, and so long as it had the healthy organic growth which was consequent on the evolution of a series of constructive problems fairly faced and in turn conquered, and again, stimulated by the growth of the Church, to which it was handmaiden, developed style after style in regular sequence, until the builders, finding they had conquered construction, took to imposing ornament. From that time, instead of ornamenting construction, they constructed ornament; and as the Reformation came to the Church in the sixteenth century so to architecture came degradation. And then the Renaissance of pagan types, from which the Gothic had derived its being by a rational development, was by the revivalists of those days hotch-potched into a more or less homogeneous mass, which even the genius of Wren could leave but coldly pedantic.

The history of the architecture of the cathedral might safely stop with the Dissolution of the Monasteries in 1538, since when it is a mere recapitulation of the doings and undoings of various sets of more or less deeply incriminated fanatics and restorers.

So that we do not feel inclined to enter into more detail, in the few remaining notes on the history of the structure.

Dean Gardiner, 1573-89, was a great reformer, and, as we have already noted, pulled down the thirteenth-century Lady Chapel, and as well the chapter-house.

In 1643 the cathedral was taken possession of by Cromwell's soldiers, and the work of spoliation carried on. The organ was probably destroyed at this time, for Dean Crofts set up a new organ in 1660, the case of which was re-modelled in 1833, and still remains. It is also perhaps needless to state that the cathedral was repeatedly whitewashed during the eighteenth century.

In June 1801 a fire broke out in the roof of the nave, but was extinguished before much damage had been done.

The various works effected during this century are mentioned specifically elsewhere in these notes, under the headings of the parts of the building where they have occurred.

Photochrom Co. Ltd., Photo.]
THE CATHEDRAL FROM THE SOUTH-WEST ANGLE OF CLOISTERS.

CHAPTER II

THE CATHEDRAL—EXTERIOR

NORWICH CATHEDRAL does not tell to great advantage from the outside: its chief charm is undoubtedly the interior. It stands in a hollow, on what is probably the lowest ground in the city. The best view of the cathedral is obtained from the low ground to the eastward near the river, and close to Pull's Ferry; here the extreme length of the nave, which Fergusson remarked justified the addition of western towers, is lost partly by foreshortening, and by the projection forward of the south transept, over which the old Norman tower, with its later battlements and spire, rises grandly above the sweep of the apse, with the still remaining circular chapels below.

The Cathedral Precincts, or Close, running from Tombland eastward to the river, are entered by two gates to the precincts and one to the bishop's palace.

The Erpingham Gate, opposite the west front of the cathedral, was built by Sir Thomas Erpingham, and as an architectural compilation "is original and unique." In elevation it consists of one lofty well-proportioned arch supported on either side by semi-hexagonal buttresses taken up as high as the apex of arch; above comes a plain gable, in which, centred over the arch below, is a canopied niche with the kneeling figure of Sir Thomas Erpingham.

Built probably about 1420, and while yet some of the noble simplicity of the thirteenth had not passed into the overwrought richness of the fifteenth and sixteenth centuries, it presents a type of the best Perpendicular work we have in England.

The form of the arch is lofty, and may have been suggested by the wish to preserve a view through of the cathedral.

The arch moulding is enriched on the outer part with figures of fourteen female saints, and on the inner with twelve male saints; the semi-hexagonal panelled buttresses are covered with the shields of the families of Erpingham, Clopton, and

Photochrom Co. Ltd., Photo.]

THE ERPINGHAM GATE.

Walton, and each has a seated figure of an ecclesiastic on the top.

The richness of this lower arch stage tells against the plain gable over, and is quite admirable in effect and defensible as a method of design; it is ornament decorating construction pure and simple, and not what later work generally was and is, constructed ornament, suggesting over-elaborate construction thereby made necessary. It will be noticed that labels with the word "Yenk" (think) sculptured thereon are placed between the shafts on either side of the archway; this has been construed "pend" by some writers, and from this the view was taken that Sir Thomas Erpingham was made to build the gate as a penance for favouring Lollardism, and that the figure of himself in the gable over the archway represents him as praying pardon for the offence.

This interpretation, however, amusing as it is, is probably erroneous, and the gate, with its shields of allied families, stands to the memory of its founder. Sir Thomas Erpingham was at Agincourt in 1415, and Shakespeare, in Act iv. of Henry V., remarks of him that he was "a knight grown grey with age and honour." Sir Thomas Browne also (p. 9 of his "Repertorium") says: "He was a Knight of the Garter in the time of Henry IV. and some part of Henry V., and I find his name in the list of the Lord Wardens of the Cinque Ports."

Sir Thomas Erpingham had two wives, Joan Clopton and Joan Walton, whose arms appear on the gateway.

St. Ethelbert's Gate, to the south, is an early "Decorated" structure. Its elevation is divided into three storeys, in the lowest of which is the gateway, with flat buttresses on each side carried up the height of two storeys, and enriched with pedimented niches in both stages. In the compartment over the arch are seven niches, four of which are pierced with windows. The upper stage is in flintwork. It was built by the citizens as part of the fine imposed on them for their share in the riots and fire of 1272 by the Court of King Henry III., though probably not until some years had elapsed, and when Edward the First had come to the throne. The upper part of the front was restored early in this century. The back elevation is interesting—the window over the arch being typical of the style.

The Gate-House forming the entrance to the bishop's palace, on the north side of the cathedral, was built by Bishop Alnwyck about 1430, and probably replaced an earlier structure; it is an interesting piece of Perpendicular work, and consists, in the lower stage, of a gate and doorway under a deep horizontal band ornamented with plain shields and mono-

[Photochrom Co. Ltd., Photo.]
ST. ETHELBERT'S GATE.

grams of the Virgin. The gateway on the left side reaches up to the horizontal bands, and has spandrels on either side; the doorway is smaller. Above are two windows with a niche between, and over all is a parapet of modern work. Flat buttresses flank the entire composition on either side. The wooden gates were added by Bishop Lyhart (1446-72).

Returning to the Erpingham gate, and entering the Close

Photochrom Co. Ltd., Photo.]
THE GATE-HOUSE OF THE BISHOP'S PALACE.

through it, immediately on our left we come to the **Chapel of St. John the Evangelist** (converted by Edward VI., and still used as a school), founded by Bishop Salmon (1299-1325). This building replaced an older structure, used as a charnel, and provision was made for this need in the new edifice; the vaults under the chapel were used for the same purpose. The porch is a later building added by Lyhart (1446-72).

The West Front of the Cathedral has probably received worse treatment than any other portion of the building, and stands now as the most unsatisfactory part of the whole. The design consists in its width of three compartments, with two separating and two flanking turrets. The centre compartment is of the width of the nave, and those on either side the width of the aisles. In the centre comes the main doorway, flanked on either side with niches, and over these, filling the entire breadth, the great nine-light west window, with the Norman turrets carried up to the base of the gable. The compartments on either side are finished off by horizontal mouldings taken across somewhat below the level of the springing of the archivolt of the main window, and have flanking turrets covered with plain pinnacles. The large west window is disproportionate, and even the assurance cheerfully given by most authorities, that it resembles the window of Westminster Hall, fails to prove that it is of suitable size here. It may be as well to note in order the various changes which have affected the west front. Mr B. W. Spaull, in Dean Goulburn's work on the Cathedral, made reference to the discovery of an alteration to the main entrance which must have been prior to that now existing. It consisted of a small *parvise* or room added above at some time subsequent to the original foundation. As the details are not now apparent, it is best to refer readers to the work named for fuller information.

The addition, however, of later Perpendicular triforium windows to the nave superimposed over the original Norman lights, which were blocked up, may have affected the west front. This can best be seen by viewing, for instance, the south side of the nave. The Norman roofs sloped down to the original triforium windows, but after the later addition were made almost flat, and must have necessitated some mask wall in the west front.

In Britton's "History of Norwich" is a drawing which is reproduced at p. 15. It will be seen that the turrets at each side of the west window are shown finished with stone cupolas, the tops of which were level with the apex of the gable. The two outside flanking turrets are shown finished by circular

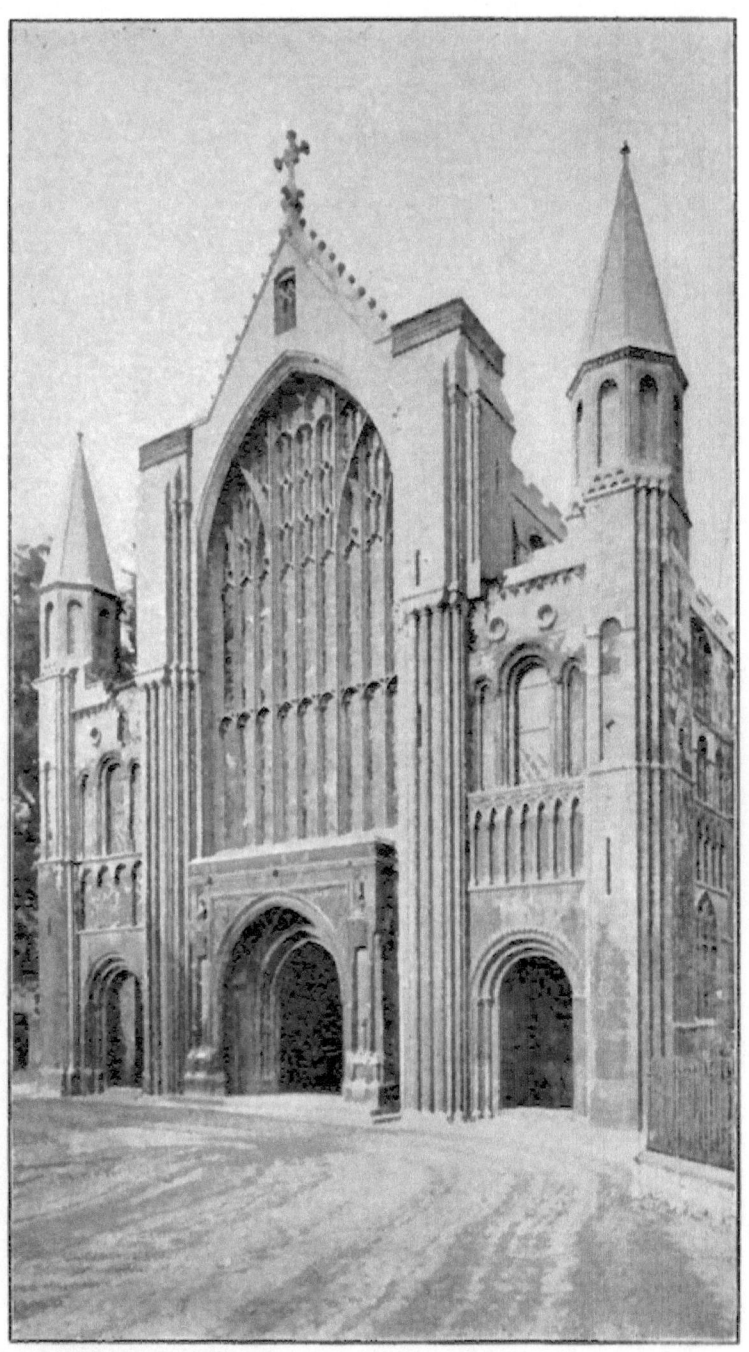

S. B. Bolas & Co., Photo.]
WEST FRONT OF THE CATHEDRAL.

drums above the parapet, and covered with leaden cupolas; these, with the Perpendicular battlements, were probably added as the mask before referred to, and necessitated by the imposition of an additional storey at the triforium level. Certainly the west front, as shown then, was better far than now. However, in 1875, "*restoration*" set in, and these cupolas were removed, and stone "pepper-box" pinnacles imposed on the turrets in their stead. The gable was restored, and the character of the work wholly destroyed, crocketted where before plain, and the niche added in the place of the small light over the vault shown in Britton's plate. In the side compartments the Perpendicular battlementing was removed and the round cannon ball holes gratuitously inserted.

The two pinnacles at the sides of the west window have since been removed.

The earlier change in the central compartment of the front from Norman to Perpendicular was effected by the additions of the door and window still remaining. Bishop Alnwyck, who was translated to Lincoln in 1436, added the doorway during his episcopate, and it was probably built right over and covering the original Norman door and arcading. He also left provision in his will for the west window, and this was added by Bishop Lyhart (1446-72), to throw additional light on to the vaulting and sculptures of the nave; from the inside it will be seen that it completely fills the width of the nave, and follows the line of the vault up.

The north side of the cathedral lies within the gardens of the bishop's palace, which can be entered from the interior of the cathedral, through a small door in the north aisle of the presbytery; the eastern end of the cathedral also lies within a private garden, but permission to enter it can usually be obtained.

Exterior of Nave.—Those portions of the precincts near the western end of the cathedral are known as the Upper Close; and, walking round the exterior of the cloisters, we come to the Lower Close. The nave on the south side can be seen well either from the upper or lower Close, and can be better examined in detail from the interior of the cloisters. Its elevation consists of fourteen bays divided by flat Norman buttresses. In height it is composed of what, at first sight, appears a bewildering confusion of arches, arcades, and windows. Over the aisle windows, hidden by the north walk of cloisters, comes a Norman wall arcading; and over this the Norman triforium windows blocked up, and again, above the later Perpendicular triforium, superimposed on the old, and finished with a battlemented parapet. Behind this come the triforium roof, and then beyond the original Norman clerestory, each bay with a triple arch formation, the centre arch pierced for a window. And then above all, the lead roof over nave vault.

The radical changes that have taken place since the nave was built by Bishop Eborard (1121-45) consist of the insertion in the aisles of later "Decorated" traceried windows in place of the original Norman ones, and of the superimposition, before referred to, at triforium level of a whole range of "Perpendicular" windows over the old Norman work, which were blocked up at this period. The pristine aspect, then, of this elevation of the nave would have shown a sloping roof over the aisles where now the later addition occurs. The battlementing, too, over the clerestory to the nave is later work, to correspond with battlementing over the triforium windows. It will be noticed that the two bays next the transept in the triforium are higher than the others, in order to throw additional light into the choir.

Also on this same south side, in the seventh and eighth bays from the west end, two very late windows occur, inserted in the Norman arcading under the original triforium windows; these were inserted by Bishop Nykke to light the chapel he built in two bays of the south aisle of the nave.

The curious raking of the lead rolls to the nave roof is noticeable; the mediæval builders did this with a view of counteracting the "crawl" of the lead. Lead, under the variations of temperature of the atmosphere, expands and contracts considerably; and from its own weight, and the steepness of the roofs, the contraction takes place in a downward direction, and starts the joints, letting in the weather. This raking of the vertical rolls was a device whereby the old builders in some measure got over their difficulty by inducing a fixed expansion and contraction.

The South Transept projects boldly forward from under the tower; without aisles, its ridge and parapet correspond in height to those of the nave; this narrowness, with the

S. B. Bolas & Co., Photo.]
THE CLERESTORY AND TRIFORIUM OF CHOIR (SOUTH SIDE).

THE CATHEDRAL—EXTERIOR

tower and spire showing over behind, gives it an appearance of height, as approached from the lower close. This effect of height is emphasised by the partition of the design in its width, by flat Norman buttresses, with shafts in the angles, and by the flat faces of the flanking turrets. The work, however, is without interest, from the fact that, though the *ensemble* in some measure has been retained, the whole of the exterior face of the stonework was re-cased by Salvin, 1830-40, during which period various restorations were effected. Before these alterations, the Norman flanking turrets finished with a "Perpendicular" battlementing, enriched with shields and quatrefoils, and with crocketted pinnacles set at the four angles; this battlementing was removed, and the present uninteresting pepper-boxes took their place. No doubt they have it in their favour that they *may* be more like the original Norman terminations than were those they replaced, which were, however, real "Perpendicular," and these are only sham Norman. Originally, from the eastward side of the south transept, projected a semi-circular chapel, shown on plan by dotted lines, and corresponding to that still remaining on the north side of the cathedral. It was part of the original plan, and though we believe no record exists of its destruction, it can safely be premised that its fate came about through the *cultus* of the saint to whom it was dedicated declining, and consequent neglect and ruin following made its destruction cheaper than its reparation. It was replaced by a sacristy in the fifteenth century, the lines of roof to which can still be seen over on the stonework. This later sacristy was destroyed by the fire of 1509, that burned as well the wooden roofs of the transepts, and necessitated the stone vaults added by Bishop Nykke.

The Diocesan Registry Offices now occupy the space on which once stood the Norman chapel, and later the Sacristy.

The building projecting eastward, south of this space, and marked A on plan, was once a chapel, said by Blomefield to have been dedicated to St. Edmund. It is now used as the **Dean's Vestry** in the lower storey, and as the **Chapter Clerk's Office** in the upper.

At the same time that the later restorations were effected to the south transept, the groined **Slype** and singing-school above it were destroyed, and the present door in the south transept from the lower close was opened. A pre-restoration view is published of the east end of the cathedral, showing the slype, in Britton's "Norwich." The visitor should also bear in mind that this space immediately in front of the south transept was originally occupied by the **Chapter-House**, situated as shown by dotted lines on plan, and separated from the cathedral by the slype. The entrance arches to the chapter-house from the east walk of the cloisters still remain and fix definitely its position; it projected eastward about eighty feet.

The Tower and Spire mark the crossing of the choir and transepts, the tower only being Norman, and square on plan, with flat Norman buttresses, covered with vertical shafts on the face of each. These buttresses start from the level of the parapets to Nave, Transept, and Presbytery, and rise right up until, well over the parapet of the tower, they are finished by crocketted pinnacles. Between these buttresses are horizontal bands of design: the lowest, a Norman arcade of nine arches, three of which are pierced as windows; then, above this, a smaller wall arcade with interlaced arches; and then, above again, the principal feature, an arcading of nine arches, three pierced for windows, and the others filled with wall tracery of diamonds and circles; then, between this last and the battlemented parapet, occur five vertical panels, each comprising two circles, the upper pierced for a window. Above, soaring upward, rises the later crocketted spire. Herbert, the founder, provided the foundations of tower, and probably carried up the walls to the level of the nave roof; the rest of the tower was finished during the reign of Henry I., and is a beautiful specimen of the work of that time; but here again our sentiment and sympathy experience a shock when we learn that the stonework was almost entirely refaced in 1856. The tower was crowned by a wooden spire from 1297; this was blown down in 1361, and probably brought away in its fall some part of the Norman turrets of the tower. It fell eastward, damaging the presbytery so badly that the clerestory had to be rebuilt. The wooden spire was reconstructed probably at the same time, though no record exists of such work, and the present Early Perpendicular turrets were added. The spire, we know, was again overtaken by misfortune in 1463, when it was struck by lightning, and again falling eastward, went through the presbytery roof. The present spire was then constructed in stone by Bishop Lyhart

THE TOWER IN 1816.

THE CATHEDRAL.—EXTERIOR

(1446-72), and was finished by his successor, Bishop Goldwell (1472-99), who added the battlements.

It will hardly be necessary to enlarge on the beauty of this spire of Norwich, as the dominant feature, seen from the south-east, rising above the curved sweep of the apse, and strongly buttressed by the south transept, it stands up, clearly defined against the western sky, and points upward, significant and symbolical at once of the ends and aspirations of the church below.

The Eastern Arm of Cathedral or Presbytery takes its history from the tower. Here, as in the nave, there are the original triforium windows blocked up, and a range of Perpendicular work superimposed on the old. Above and beyond this, supported between each bay by flying buttresses, comes the transitional Decorated to Perpendicular clerestory, considerably higher than the original Norman clerestory remaining to the nave. At the base of each flying buttress are figures of saints. The roof and Norman clerestory were damaged by the falling tower in 1361, but were rebuilt by Bishop Percy, 1355-69. This work is transitional Decorated to Perpendicular. The presbytery was then re-roofed with a framed timber construction, which was consumed by the falling of the burning spire, struck by lightning in 1463. The present stone vault was added in its place by Bishop Goldwell, 1472-99. This necessitated the addition as well of flying buttresses to take the thrust of the vault.

The battlementing to the presbytery also was added at the same time as the flying buttresses.

It will also be noted that here, as in the nave, an addition was made in the way of a range of later "Perpendicular" windows superimposed over the original Norman triforium, which was blocked up.

The Chapel of St. Mary-the-Less, marked B on plan, projects southward from the presbytery, and dates from the fourteenth century. Between this and the circular Norman chapel of St. Luke, was Bishop Wakeryng's chapel. It has long since disappeared, but the doorway of Perpendicular design remained until about 1841, when it was removed and the compartment Normanised — a piece of wanton vandalism and the destruction of an historical link.

The circular Norman chapels, of which two remain, are

very interesting. In the original plan of the founder there were three; but the easternmost was superseded by Early English structure, which in its turn was demolished.

The Chapel of Saint Luke, marked c on plan, flanking the south side of the apse, was much restored in the sixties; in Britton's "Norwich," published in 1816, late "Decorated" windows are shown; these were replaced by *modern* Norman. Its form is peculiar; on plan, that of two circles interpenetrating. On elevation, in the lower stage, are the modern Norman windows, with shafts in jambs, over which occur two tiers of arcading, in the higher of which window openings are pierced. The position of the Norman Lady Chapel is shown by dotted lines, as well as the rectangular shape of the Early English chapel built by Walter de Suffield (1245-57) about 1250. The line of the roof of the later chapel can still be seen plainly traced on the stonework over the arches which once gave entrance to it. This later chapel was destroyed by Dean Gardiner in Queen Elizabeth's reign. The foundations of both chapels have been laid open quite recently but a few feet under the level of the garden.

The Jesus Chapel, marked D on plan, on the north side of the apse, retains the early "Perpendicular" windows inserted in the Norman work; its other characteristics are as those described to St. Luke's Chapel in the south.

On the north side of the presbytery, and to the west of the Jesus Chapel, were other chapels, shown on the plan by dotted lines; the positions of their roofs are clearly marked yet on the stonework. One must have been the **Reliquary Chapel**; the bridge chapel in the north aisle of presbytery formed its ante-chapel.

The North Transept, and generally the north side of the cathedral, are more conveniently examined from the gardens of the bishop's palace, whence this portion of the exterior of the cathedral can best be seen.

The details of the fabric on the north side are essentially the same as those described to the south side of cathedral; though here the work has been less restored, and consequently is of more interest to the student. The original Norman chapel, now used as a store-house, projects eastward from the north transept; a corresponding feature occurred in the south transept, but has long since vanished.

S. B. Bolas & Co., Photo.]
THE EXTERIOR OF THE CHAPEL OF ST. LUKE FROM THE EAST.

The Bishop's Palace stands to the north of the cathedral, and was formerly connected with it by a vaulted passage. Herbert, the founder, built the first palace, of which portions are incorporated in the present building. Bishop Salmon (1299-1325) in 1318, according to the patent rolls of the twelfth year of the reign of Edward II., obtained licence to buy a piece of land 47 perches 4 feet in length, and 23 perches 12 feet in breadth, to enlarge and rebuild thereon the palace of Herbert. He also built a chapel, and the great hall, measuring 120 feet from north to south, and 60 feet wide, with kitchen, buttery, and offices at the west end. The grand ruin somewhat to the east of the palace now is supposed to have formed part of the entrance to this hall. It was, however, too large to keep up, and so was leased by Bishop Nykke, just before his death in 1535 to the mayor, sheriff, and citizens, so that the Guild of S. George might hold their annual feast there. Later on it became a meeting-house. The present private chapel of the bishop was built by Bishop Reynolds in 1662 across part of the south end.

To the north of the nave of the cathedral, and on the west side of the palace, was an open area called the *green-yard*, and in Sir Thomas Browne's "Works," vol. iv. p. 27 (London, 1835) is an account of the *combination sermons* which were preached here in the summer prior to the Reformation.

"Before the late times the combination sermons were preached, in the summer time, at the Cross in the Green Yard where there was a good accommodation for the auditors. The mayor, aldermen, with their wives and officers, had a well-contrived place built against the wall of the Bishop's palace, covered with lead, so that they were not offended by rain. Upon the north side of the church, places were built gallery wise, one above another, where the dean, prebends and their wives, gentlemen, and the better sort, very well heard the sermon: the rest either stood or sat in the green, upon long forms provided for them, paying a penny or half-penny a-piece, as they did at S. Paul's Cross in London. The Bishop and chancellor heard the sermons at the windows of the Bishop's palace: the pulpit had a large covering of lead over it, and a cross upon it; and there were eight or ten stairs of stone about it, upon which the hospital boys and others stood. The preacher had his face to the south, and there was a painted board of a foot and a half broad and about a yard and a half long hanging over his head, before, upon which were painted the names of the benefactors towards the Combination Sermon which he particularly commemorated in his prayer. . . ."

On the north side of the cathedral, in the seventh compartment of the aisle from the west end, the walled-up entrance to the *green-yard* is to be noticed.

There is no doubt that this space was originally the cemetery of the monks, and Harrod quotes from the *Chronicle* of John de Whethamsted to that effect. A stone coffin lid found here in 1848 goes to confirm this.

CHAPTER III

THE INTERIOR

NORWICH CATHEDRAL is justly celebrated for the beauty of its interior. Entering from the upper close by the north aisle door, and then taking a position immediately under the great west window, facing east, there is before one the long perspective of the Norman nave, the choir and presbytery, while overhead comes the later vault, telling richly by contrast with the severe plainness of the earlier work below. The extreme length of the cathedral is about 407 feet. The nave, always long in Norman churches, is here over 200 feet from the west door to the choir screen. Although some critics object to the position of the organ on this same screen, there can be no doubt that, not only is it a most admirable position for the instrument acoustically, but also that its presence here does not detract from the general effect of the interior. From the west end of the nave, as a dark silhouette against the eastern apsidal windows, or as an object in the middle distance, it helps the spectator to realise the length of the cathedral. A certain sense of mystery and something undiscerned adds to the charm of an interior, and the organ here helps, with the screen, to enshrine the eastern arm and most sacred portion of the building, and interrupts the vista for the sake of which disastrous sacrifices have been made in many of our cathedral churches.

The Nave consists of seven double bays; in all, fourteen compartments from the west end to the tower crossing.

It will be noticed that, in the plan (page 113), a square of the nave, occupying longitudinally the space of two bays of the aisles, is indicated by the dotted lines; also a main pier is marked as Y and a subsidiary pier as Z.

The main piers, as at Y, are large rectangular masses, having on the nave side a flat buttress-like piece added, with shafts in the angles, and bearing on the face the two vaulting shafts. On the aisle side are two shafts to each transverse arch; and on the two lateral faces are triple shafts to the arcade arches, with four angle shafts at each corner of the main pier, taking the outer rings to same. The plan is the same at the triforium level. The smaller or subsidiary piers (as at x) have single vaulting shafts on the nave face, double ones to the aisle, and under the arcade arches convex faces, with four angle shafts, as in main piers. The plan of these piers determines the elevation. The nave arcade arches, ornamented with the billet, and triforium with a *chevron* or zig-zag, are almost equal in size, and over these lower stages comes the typical triple Norman clerestory with walk; the whole covered in by the fine lierne vault.

A NORMAN CAPITAL.
(From a Drawing by the Author.)

The vault has thirteen complete bays and two semi-bays, one at either end. The junctions between this later vault and the Norman work can be seen. The main piers had the original double shafts cut off at the level of the top of the triforium arches, the later single shaft being brought down and joined by a peculiar branch-like connection. The original shafts to the subsidiary piers, which it is probable took only a minor part in carrying the flat Norman wooden roof, were finished by a cap at the impost level of the triforium, and the later shaft was brought down and finished by the *rebus* of Bishop Lyhart, the constructor of the vault. This *rebus* should be noticed; it is a pun in stone, with its hart lying in water.

It will also be noticed that the outer arches of the triforium are not concentric with the sub-arches.

Photochrom Co. Ltd., Photo.]
THE NAVE, LOOKING EAST.

The bases of the shafts have been Perpendicularised, probably when the vault was added, and the Norman character of the lateral shafts spoilt by scraping.

The building of the nave is usually attributed to Bishop Eborard (1121-45), but some eminent archæologists believe that the whole cathedral, nave and all, was built by Herbert, 1091-1119, the first bishop and founder. We believe there is no documentary evidence against this theory. The *Registrum Primum* says: "Moreover, the same Herbert completed the church of Norwich in his own time, as I have learned from the account of old people, *but have not found in writing*, as far as the altar of the holy cross, which is now called the altar of S. William."

The billet enrichment on the main arches, and the chevron or zig-zag on those of the triforium, have been looked upon as indicating that this part of the building—the five western bays of nave—is later than the presbytery, the arches there lacking this ornament. But as these are quite the earliest forms of ornament used by the Norman builders, their occurrence here at Norwich cannot prove much. It is better perhaps to reserve judgment, and be content with merely stating the facts and the more generally accredited theories as to the age of the western part of the nave.

The subsidiary circular columns in the fifth bay of the nave from the west end should be noticed. A small enriched shaft in the clerestory of the north transept is here illustrated. This very beautiful style of treatment was common to the Norman builder, with the Romanesque, and the Romans before them.

The Choir Screen crosses the nave between the subsidiary piers to the sixth bay. Of the original work erected by Bishop Lyhart, 1446-72, the sub-structure of the present screen is the only portion remaining. Traces of two altars, one on either side of the doorway, can still be seen; these were originally dedicated to St. William of Norwich and St. Mary. These altars were enclosed in chapels formed by screens coming forward to the extent of half the bay, and stopped against the main nave piers on either side—the double vaulting shafts on the face of which are stopped by corbels, carved as heads, at about the height that the chapels would have reached. They were vaulted over, and above came the rood loft and organ. The rood loft was damaged by the Puritans, and probably removed after the Restoration. Dean Crofts, in 1660, set up a new organ.

In Britton's "Norwich," 1816, the upper stage of the choir screen is shown divided into square panels, occurring vertically over the lower stage; the screens to the chapels before referred to having been destroyed. In 1833 Salvin remodelled the choir, and turned his attention to the choir screen: the organ was placed in its present position, and cased with the frame of that instrument which Dean Crofts had set up in 1660; and the overhanging vault to the screen was added.

The Nave Vault (height 72 feet), which was added by Bishop Lyhart, 1446-72, took the place of the original Norman wooden roof destroyed by fire in 1463. This earlier Norman roof was most probably like that now existing at Peterborough, and was no doubt profusely decorated with colour. The vault is of Perpendicular design, and known as *lierne*; such vaults may be distinguished by the fact that between the main ribs, springing from the vaulting shafts, are placed cross ribs forming a pattern, as it were, and bracing the main ribs, but not in any great measure structural. This vault at Norwich may be taken as typical of the last legitimate development of the stone roof; it was the precursor of the later fan vaulting, such as we find in Henry VII.'s chapel at Westminster, where legitimate construction was replaced by ostentatious ingenuity and the accumulation of needless ornament and detail.

The carved bosses here at Norwich, occurring at the intersection of the ribs, are worth careful study. Those who care to go into the matter in the fullest detail should consult Dean Goulburn's book published in 1876, which not only gives an admirable history of the fabric and the See, but enters fully into the detail and symbolic meaning of each of the 328 bosses.

In this list, compiled from that volume, mention is made only of those bosses on the main longitudinal rib of the vault; it is hoped that this method will enable the visitor to readily enter into the meaning of any group of bosses, by providing a keynote to the whole. The subjects are taken from Bible history, and each epoch is usually grouped around some central incident figured on the main longitudinal ribs. In each bay No. 4 is the large central boss.

S. B. Bolas & Co., Photo.]
THE CHOIR SCREEN AND ORGAN FROM THE NAVE.

The Easternmost Bay.—No. 1.

(1.) The Creation of Light. (2.) A Figure of the Almighty.
(3.) A White Hart. (4.) The Temptation.
(5.) A White Swan. (6.) The Death of Cain.

The Second Bay.—No. 2.

(1.) Cain driven out as a Fugitive. (2.) Noah building the Ark.
(3.) Noah's Drunkenness. (4.) The Ark on the Waters.
(5.) Meaning indefinite. (6.) Noah planting the Vine.

The Third Bay.—No. 3.

(1.) The Building of the Tower of Babel. (2.) The Tower of Babel shown as Feudal Fortress.
(3.) Abraham entertaining an Angel. (4.) Abraham sacrificing Isaac.
(5.) Jacob deceiving Isaac. (6.) Isaac blessing Esau.

The Fourth Bay.—No. 4.

(1.) Sarah at the Door of Abraham's House. (2.) Jacob going to Padan-Aram.
(3.) Jacob wrestling with the Angel. (4.) Jacob pilling the Green Poplar Rods.
(5.) Jacob's Ladder. (6.) Jacob making the Covenant with Laban.

The Fifth Bay.—No. 5.

(1.) Jacob sending Joseph to his Brethren. (2.) Joseph journeying to his Brethren.
(3.) Joseph stripped of his Coat of Many Colours. (4.) Joseph cast into the Pit.
(5.) Joseph sold to the Ishmaelite Merchants. (6.) Joseph set up over the Egyptians.

The Sixth Bay.—No. 6.

(1.) Joseph selling corn. (2.) Moses in the Ark of Bulrushes.
(3.) The Angel appearing to Moses in the Burning Bush. (4.) The Overthrow of the Egyptians in the Red Sea.
(5.) The Ark of the Covenant. (6.) Samson rending the Lion.

The Seventh Bay.—No. 7.

(1.) Samson taking the Gates of the City of Gaza. (2.) David smiting Goliath.
(3.) David cutting off Goliath's Head. (4.) David crowned.
(5.) David charging Solomon. (6.) Solomon enthroned.

The Eighth Bay.—No. 8.

(1.) Solomon enthroned. (2.) The Annunciation.
(3.) The Presentation in the Temple. (4.) The Nativity.
(5.) The Visitation. (6.) Herod decreeing the Massacre of the Innocents.

The Ninth Bay.—No. 9.

(1.) The Flight into Egypt.
(2.) Christ in the midst of the Doctors.
(3.) The Marriage in Cana of Galilee.
(4.) The Baptism of Our Lord.
(5.) The Raising of Lazarus.
(6.) The Supper in Bethany.

The Tenth Bay.—No. 10.

(1.) Christ's Entry into Jerusalem.
(2.) Circular Hole for Descent of Thurible.
(3.) Our Lord sending forth the Disciples.
(4.) The Last Supper.
(5.) Disciples preparing for the Foot-washing.
(6.) Our Lord washing Peter's Feet.

The Eleventh Bay.—No. 11.

(1.) Our Lord in Gethsemane.
(2.) Christ crowned with Thorns.
(3.) Christ led to Pilate.
(4.) Christ before Pilate.
(5.) Christ Blindfolded.
(6.) Christ Betrayed.

The Twelfth Bay.—No. 12.

(1.) Christ taken to the House of the High Priest.
(2.) Christ nailed to the Cross.
(3.) The Soldiers casting Lots.
(4.) The Crucifixion.
(5.) The Entombment.
(6.) Christ in Hades.

The Thirteenth Bay.—No. 13.

(1.) Soldiers watching the Holy Sepulchre.
(2.) The Resurrection.
(3.) Three Apostles.
(4.) The Ascension.
(5.) The Virgin praying.
(6.) The Day of Pentecost.

The Fourteenth Bay.—No. 14.

(1.) A Miracle of Exorcism.
(2.) The Jaws of Hell.
(3.) The Drunkard's Doom.
(4.) The Last Judgment.
(5.) St. Peter.
(6.) The Holy Trinity.
(7.) Bishop Lyhart, the Builder of the Vault.

To all those who take an interest in early stone cutting, this vault of Norwich is a store of inexhaustible treasure; the bosses, rudely cut as they are, tell their own tales with singular truth and directness. Their sculpture may not display the anatomical knowledge of the work of the Renaissance; yet it has a distinct decorative value that has been seldom equalled in the later decadent period. The fourteen large central bosses on the main longitudinal ribs present

THE INTERIOR

in themselves an epitome not only of Bible history, but of the connecting incidents forming the theme of Christian teaching. In the tenth bay, on the longitudinal rib, there is, in place of a boss, a circular hole through the vault. It is supposed to have been formed to allow a thurible to be suspended therefrom into the church below. Harrod, quoting from Lambard's "Topographical Dictionary," says: "I myself, being a child, once saw in Poule's Church at London, at a feast of Whitsontide, wheare the comyng down of the Holy Gost was set forth by a white pigeon that was let to fly *out of a hole that is yet to be seen in the mydst of the roof of the great ile,* and by a long censer which, descending out of the same place almost to the very ground, was swinged up and down at such a length that it reached at one swepe *almost to the west gate of the church, and with the other to the queer [quire] stairs of the same,* breathing out over the whole church and companie a most pleasant perfume of such sweet things as burned therein."

It is probable that the hole in the nave vault at Norwich was used for a similar purpose; and its position would seem to agree with such use, situated as it is about midway between the west end and where the front of the mediæval rood loft occurred.

The West Window, added, as we have already noted by Bishop Lyhart, to light the vault, resembles that of Westminster Hall in the lines of its tracery; the glass by Hedgeland constitutes a memorial to Bishop Stanley (d. 1849).

West Door.—The original Norman arch remains over the doorway on the inside.

The North Aisle of Nave, the Norman windows of which were entirely replaced by Decorated ones, is covered by plain quadri-partite vaults. In the triforium over, as previously noted in description of exterior, the side walls were raised, the original Norman windows blocked up and Perpendicular ones placed over, the roof being at the same time raised on the outside to the necessary height, and made of a shallower pitch; this is clearly noticeable from the triforium walks.

In the easternmost bays, two windows were raised still more to gain additional light for the choir.

In the seventh bay from the west end occurs the door once leading to the *green yard*.

The South Aisle of Nave corresponds with the north, and is covered with a plain quadri-partite vault, with the

S. B. Bolas & Co., Photo.]
THE NORTH AISLE OF NAVE, LOOKING WEST.

exception of the seventh and eighth bays from the west; these were converted by Bishop Nykke into a chapel enclosed by screens, and are marked on the plan as F.E. The Norman vaults were here removed and the late Perpendicular ones constructed in their stead; the windows appear to be of still later date, but are supposed to have been, and most probably were, inserted at this period.

Monuments in Nave.—The nave suffered severely at the hands of the Puritans, who destroyed many of the early tombs and effigies. Especially noticeable is the lack of brasses; all these have disappeared, with the exception only of one in the Jesus Chapel. Another singularity is that the burial-place of most of the bishops who are known to have been interred in the cathedral is quite uncertain. The best of them seem to have been content with a plain slab and inscribed brass; only Nykke, of infamous memory, left so gorgeous a chapel behind to perpetuate it.

Bishop Hall, in his "Hard Measure," gives a sketch of vivid historical interest of the sacrilege committed during the Puritan rebellion, and when, in 1643, the cathedral was in the possession of the fanatics. "Lord, what work was here, what clattering of glasses, what beating down of Walls, what tearing up of Monuments, what pulling down of Seates, what wresting out of Irons and Brass from the Windows and Graves! What defacing of Armes, what demolishing of curious stone work, that had not any representation in the World, but only of the cost of the Founder and skill of the Mason, what toting and piping upon the destroyed Organ pipes, and what a hideous triumph on the Market day before all the Countrey, when, in a kind of Sacrilegious and profane procession, all the Organ pipes, Vestments, both Copes and Surplices, together with the Leaden Crosse which had been newly sawne down from over the Green-Yard Pulpit, and the Service books and singing books that could be had, were carried to the fire in the publick Market place; A leud wretch walking before the Train, in his Cope trailing in the dirt, with a Service book in his hand, imitating in an impious scorne the tune, and usurping the words of the Letany; neer the Publick Crosse, all these monuments of Idolatry must be sacrificed to the fire, not without much Ostentation of a zealous joy."

Monuments in North Aisle of Nave.—In the fifth bay of the nave arcade (marked 1 on plan) is the altar tomb of Sir Thomas Wyndham and his four wives. This was

58 NORWICH CATHEDRAL.

originally in the Lady Chapel, then, for a time, the Jesus Chapel, and about 1869 moved to its present position.

Between the sixth and seventh bay is buried Dean Prideaux (d. 1724). The ninth bay of aisle is lighted by a memorial window to William Smith (d. 1849), Professor of Modern History at Cambridge. In the tenth bay (marked

Photochrom Co. Ltd., Photo.]
THE EAST WALK OF THE CLOISTERS.

2 on plan) is the altar tomb, with panelled sides, to Sir John Hobart (d. 1507), Attorney-General to Henry VII.

Monuments in South Aisle of Nave from the west.—In the sixth bay is a memorial window by Wailes to members of the Hales family. In the seventh bay (marked 3 on plan) is the tomb of Chancellor Spencer; the rents of the dean and chapter were formerly paid here. The ninth bay (marked 4 on plan) contains the altar tomb of Bishop Parkhurst (1560-74).

The Cloisters and destroyed monastic buildings.—The

cloisters are on the south side of the cathedral, the interior garth being about 145 feet square.

The original Norman cloisters, which were probably of a wooden construction, were destroyed by the fire of 1272; and the work of building the present cloisters was commenced by Bishop Walpole (1289-99) about 1297, but they were not completely finished until 1430, in the time of Bishop Alnwyck (1426-36). They present an interesting, and, at the same time, complex study of the development of the styles during the one hundred and thirty-three years which passed during their erection; a paper by the Rev. D. J. Stewart (published in vol. 32 of the *Archæological Journal*) goes minutely into their construction, and the several parts the various bishops of Norwich played in their design. Those who wish to study this part of the cathedral thoroughly cannot do better than refer to this paper.

It will be noticed that, despite the lengthy period occupied in the construction of the cloisters, the result is in no way inharmonious; it is only in the detail, and especially the open tracery to the bays, that the difference of style is very perceptible.

Counting the angle severies as in each walk, it will be noticed that there are fourteen severies on the east side; and thirteen on the other three. Each is nearly square on plan, and vaulted over with horizontal longitudinal and transverse ribs, between which occur diagonals and *tiercerons*; with carved bosses at the intersections. The piers carrying the vaults consist of groups of separate cylindrical shafts of Purbeck marble.

On the three sides—east, west, and south—there are separate storeys of apartments over the vaults, which were used for various purposes by the monks.

In elevation—and of course this can best be seen from the Garth—each bay is divided by a projecting buttress with diagonal one in the angles; the arches are filled with open tracery carried by two mullions; it is this tracery which marks most clearly the various changes of style. The shape of the arch is similar throughout. This was a concession on the part of the later builders which ensured harmony in the whole; but on each side the tracery is varied. On the east side it is geometrical in character, the work being transitional between

Early English and Decorated; on the south side the tracery is more flowing and has advanced to Decorated; on the west side again, we get the transitional style between Decorated and Perpendicular, with some *flamboyant* or flame-like detail; while on the north and latest side it is frankly Perpendicular.

The East Walk of cloisters is the earliest; access to which is gained from the south aisle of nave of cathedral, through the **Prior's Door**; of this fine specimen of early Decorated work we give an illustration. In the sixth bay, from, and counting the angle, may be seen the walled-up entrance to the Slype. In the seventh, eighth, and ninth bays remain the arches which once gave entrance to the chapter-house; these were walled up until about 1850.

According to the itinerary of William of Worcester, the chapter-house, which was built by Bishop Walpole (1289-99), projected eastward about 80 feet, terminating with a polygonal apse, as shown by the dotted lines to our plan.

The prolongation of this east walk southwards beyond the south walk of the cloisters, led formerly to the infirmary; of which now only remain the three piers in the lower close; the greater part having been pulled down in 1804. During some time in the eighteenth century the infirmary was used as a workhouse.

The dormitories in all monasteries were connected with one of the transepts, usually the south, so that the monks could at all hours easily gain access to the cathedral for the performance of the offices of their order; it is probable, therefore, that the rooms over this east walk of the cloisters here at Norwich may have been used as dormitories, with a staircase on the western side of the south transept leading to them. The dormitories are supposed by some antiquarians to have been placed south of the destroyed chapter-house; the door in the twelfth bay of the east wall of the cloisters (marked 5 on plan) probably giving rise to the supposition.

The sculptured vault-bosses in this walk are illustrative of incidents in Gospel story and of the legends of the four evangelists.

The South Walk, the south wall of which was also the wall of the refectory. A door (marked 6 on plan) at the western end of this walk led to the refectory. To the west were probably the kitchen and offices. The sculptured bosses of

the vault over this walk are illustrations of scenes from the
Book of Revelation.

THE PRIOR'S DOOR.
[After a Drawing by S. K. Greenslade.

The West Walk.—In the first two bays (marked 7 on
plan) are the lavatories of the monks; and in the fourth bay, a

door (marked 8 on plan) that formerly led to the guest hall, pulled down by Dean Gardiner, 1573-89. The cellarer whose duty it was to look after the guests probably had apartments above.

A door in the last bay leads to the **Choir School**; this was formerly the **Locutory,** where the monks indulged in their daily gossip. The western wall is in the Early Decorated style; the body of the room dating from Norman times.

The door into the south aisle of the cathedral from this walk, known as the **Monks' Door,** is of an elaborate example of the Perpendicular style.

Returning along the **North Walk,** the latest part of the cloisters, we come again to the prior's door, by entering which the rest of the interior may be inspected.

The Ante-choir occupies one compartment of the nave, and is immediately under the organ loft. It was in mediæval times a chapel dedicated to Our Lady of Pity. The screens between this ante-choir and the aisles on north and south, were in part formed from the Perpendicular screen which originally divided off the Jesus Chapel from the north aisle of the presbytery. Here in the ante-choir they are certainly preferable, even as "mutilated Perpendicular," to any modern substitute; though it was lamentable vandalism to remove them from their original positions, where they are shown in Britton's "History."

The Choir.—It may be as well here to give a brief sketch of the various re-modellings which have been effected in the arrangement of the choir and presbytery of the cathedral.

Britton shows, in one of his plates published in 1816, the floor of the choir continued at its level until, immediately before the altar, in the apse, it rises by five steps to the level of the sanctuary (the presbytery, after the Reformation, had been cut off from the choir by a wooden screen, in front of which stood the communion table). Across both transepts, in the beginning of the century, there stood cumbrous two-storeyed structures containing pews not unlike boxes at a theatre, as shown in a drawing here reproduced. In 1837, when Salvin re-modelled the choir, these were removed, and on the south side replaced by a stone gallery, and this again has been taken down.

In Dean Goulburn's time the floor of the presbytery was raised by two steps, which occurred one bay past the tower arch eastward.

S. B. Bolas & Co., Photo.]

THE CHOIR AND PRESBYTERY.

THE INTERIOR

Quite recently, there have been further alterations carried out by Dean Lefroy. The eastern arm of the building was closed for two and a half years, and during this time the whole of the whitewash, etc., covering the stonework was flaked off, with much benefit to the appearance of this part of the interior. The level of the presbytery floor has been brought forward to the tower arch, and at the same time the floors of both transepts and choir were brought to one level, and various obstructions in the way of pews and raised floors removed.

The choir was opened after this work by Archbishop Benson, 2nd May 1894.

The Choir extends one bay, or the space of two compartments, into the nave, as was usual in cathedral priories, and was originally occupied during the offices of the Benedictines by the prior, sub-prior, and the sixty monks. The bishop — who was the nominal abbot — with his presbyters, occupied the presbytery.

The stalls, sixty in number, with an additional two for the prior and sub-prior, facing east, are fine specimens of fifteenth-century work, the detail varying though the main lines are preserved in each.

Each of these stalls retains the *subsellium* or *miserere*, which, hinged at the back, turns up and discloses a small ledge beneath supported by carving, which ledge is supposed to have been used by the aged monks to rest on during the first long office of the Benedictines, which lasted four

A STALL IN THE CHOIR.
(After a Drawing by
S. K. Greenslade.)

hours. Did they, however, by any chance allow the seat to fall, they are said to have had to go through the whole of their prayers again as a penance. All these *misereres* are worth studying, especially as the white and grey paint which had disfigured them has been cleaned off since 1806.

The choir was re-arranged by Salvin in 1833, and the chancellor's stall, shown in early prints, against the north-east tower pier, was removed at this time. The presbytery was filled with stalls, which have been lately removed, and in part refixed in the nave. During the recent alterations the row of fifteenth-century stalls, each with its *miserere*, has been removed from its original position in front of the canopied stalls, and placed across the transepts, and their place taken by others, made up of various fragments of old seating.

Also the older bishop's throne, erected by Dean Lloyd late in the eighteenth century, "in resemblance to ancient Gothic workmanship," was removed from the south-east pier of the tower and placed in the consistory court, and its place taken (1894) by the present erection, designed by Pearson also in the style of ancient Gothic workmanship, and made by Cornish and Gaymer. The new pulpit, taking the place of that put up after the demolition of the chancellor's stall, was designed by J. D. Seddon, and executed by H. Hems of Exeter.

The Pelican Lectern, now in the choir (see illustration, p. 110), was formerly hidden away in the Jesus Chapel; it is late Decorated in character; the three small figures were added in 1845. There is enough metal in this piece of mediæval work to make a dozen modern replicas.

The Presbytery consists of two double severies, or four compartments, terminated by a semi-circular apse of five compartments. The four compartments on either side have, in the lower stages of their design, rich four-centred arches of Perpendicular period, with niches between on the piers; the spandrels are filled in to a horizontal line, above which, at the level of the triforium floor, is an elaborate cusped cresting. The triforium is Norman, lofty in scale. Over this come four light transitional (Decorated to Perpendicular) clerestory windows, with niches canopied forward in the thickness of the wall over the clerestory path; the windows being on the outer face of wall. From the apex of the ogee arches of the niches spring the vaulting ribs of the later vault, without

THE CHOIR AND PRESBYTERY IN 1816.

any intermediate shaft. The apse preserves its Norman characteristics in the lower stage as well as at the triforium level. Here the interest of the student must surely be concentrated; as this eastern arm of the cathedral is the earliest part of the building. Herbert, the founder, laid the foundation-stone at the extreme east, probably in the original Norman Lady Chapel, and built westwards, and here, in front of the high altar, was he buried.

The remains of the first bishop's throne, with the westward position, are in the central bay of the apse. Behind it, in the screen wall, can be discerned an arch which looks like a door head; if there be a vault beneath the presbytery, it is probable that this is the walled-up entrance.

On the east side of the tower over the arch can be seen the lines of the original Norman roof. The Norman clerestory was so badly damaged by part of the tower falling in 1362 that the present clerestory was built in its place by Bishop Percy (1355-69), the presbytery, at the same time being covered over with a framed timber roof. In 1463 this (together with the spire) was struck by lightning, and fell burning into the presbytery, where it burned itself away. Here and there in the aisles, and wherever the Norman stonework is visible, traces of an orange discoloration give evidence of the heat generated by the mass.

The present lierne vault was added by Bishop Goldwell (1472-99), and his rebus, a gold well, can be seen cut on the bosses at the intersections of vaulting ribs. The curious junction of the later vault with the ogee-shaped arches of the clerestory should be noticed.

While the original triforium yet remains, the character of the main arcade was altered by the insertion of the four-centred "Perpendicular" arches, the work of Bishop Goldwell, whose tomb is under one on the south side. These lower arches were filled with screens, removed in 1875.

The lower apsidal arches, in the beginning of the century, were completely filled with imitation Norman work; this has been cleared away to the original height of the screen wall, with much improvement to the general effect.

The present altar, designed by Sir A. W. Blomfield, occupies probably the position of the original altar. The question where the high altar stood has provoked much speculation.

THE CHOIR STALLS AT THE BEGINNING OF THE NINETEENTH CENTURY.

Professor Willis placed it more to the westward, thinking that a quatrefoiled opening or hagioscope in the screen wall of the last bay on the north side of the Presbytery (marked 9 on plan) was made to afford a view of it from the aisle. Harrod points out that there is a small hole in the vault above, from which probably hung down the light of the sacrament. The position of this hole, and the fact that such a light would necessarily be placed before the altar, and not over or behind it, is evidence that the altar was about where it is now. Blomfield, again, averred that the people stood in the aisle and confessed to the priest standing in the sanctuary, the "voice coming through a hole made in the wall for that purpose," the hole being the hagioscope referred to. But, as Harrod observes, to do this the priest must have assumed a recumbent position, which is neither convenient nor usual.

The real use, no doubt, of this bay of the arcade, was for the Easter sepulchre; its usual position is on the north side of the sanctuary. It will be noticed also that in the aisle immediately behind is a raised gallery of Decorated character, access to which was gained from the sanctuary by steps on the left side of the bay of the arcade, in which occurs the hagioscope. This gallery formed the ante-chapel to the **Reliquary Chapel**, which projected northwards from the aisle of the cathedral; the roof line of this chapel can be seen plainly from the outside. From the reliquary chapel on Good Friday the crucifix and pyx were taken out and deposited in the Easter sepulchre below; and from the vault above, through the hole before referred to, was hung the great sepulchre light. More probably the hagioscope was intended to be used by the watcher at the sepulchre.

The arrangement of the presbytery, as we have already noted when referring to the plates here reproduced from Britton, has undergone many changes; in the beginning of the century the level of the floor of the choir was continued until between the third and fourth bay from the tower in the presbytery, where it rose by five steps to the level of the sanctuary floor. Harrod speaks of two steps up at the third pier past the tower, and three at the fourth or point of the junction of the apse. In Dean Goulburn's time, the sanctuary space was enlarged by being brought forward one bay. The present floor, designed by Sir A. W. Blomfield in glass mosaic and porphyry, was executed by Powell Brothers. Then also was added the somewhat elaborate communicants'

S. B. Bolas & Co., Photo.]
THE CHOIR, LOOKING WEST.

rail, executed in bronze and spars. In enlarging the sanctuary, Dean Goulburn moved the three steps from the fourth pier past the tower to the third, and at the same time the two steps at the third pier were moved forward to the first past the tower. And now again, during the recent works of reparation, the presbytery floor has been brought forward at one level to the tower arch, where it descends to the level of the choir floor by five steps: screens which filled the first bays on either side were removed, and similar flights of steps now descend from the presbytery and the north and south aisles. The cumbrous stalls were also removed, and in part refixed in the nave.

The stained glass which fills the clerestory windows of the apse dates from 1846, and was made by Yarrington. The window in the triforium just above the altar contains modern stained-glass, dedicated to the memory of Canon Thurlow.

Monuments in the Presbytery.—The monument of Herbert, the first bishop of Norwich, and the founder of the cathedral, was raised in the centre of presbytery, before the high altar. It was so much injured during the time of the Rebellion that a new one was erected in 1682; this again was levelled, and a slab placed in the floor at the same place now remains.

In the second bay eastward from the tower (south side), marked 10 on plan. Bishop Goldwell's (1472-99) chantry, and the altar tomb, remarkable for the effigy in full pontificals (see illustration). Bloxam remarks that it is "the only instance of the monumental effigy of a bishop, prior to the Reformation, in which the *cappa pluvialis*, or processional cope, is represented as the outward vestment instead of the casula or chesible." The tomb is placed to the south of the recess; in the space east was an altar.

In the third bay eastward was Bishop Wakering's (1416-25) tomb, the only part of which now remaining is visible from the south aisle, and consists of a series of panels with plain shields and figures two by two, with the several instruments of the Passion. There were formerly steps down into the south aisle from this bay. In the same place is a monument to Bishop Overall (d. 1619).

In the fourth bay (marked 11 on plan) the altar tomb of Sir William Boleyn of Blickling (d. 1505).

Of the fourth bay eastward from tower on the south side (marked 9 on plan), Sir Thomas Browne says: "On the north of the choir—*the presbytery is meant*—between the two arches,

DETAIL OF THE PRESBYTERY CLERESTORY AND VAULTING.
[After a Drawing by S. K. Greenslade.

next to Queen Elizabeth's seat, were buried Sir Thomas Erpingham and his wives, the Lady Joan, etc., whose pictures were in the painted glass windows next to this place, with the arms of the Erpinghams. The insides of both the pillars were painted in red colours, with divers figures and inscriptions from the top almost to the bottom, which are now washed out by the late whiting of the pillars. . . . There was a long brass inscription about the tombstone, which was torn away in the late times, the name of Erpingham only remaining."

During the recent works, under this same spot was found a leaden coffin enclosing human bones, which were possibly the remains of Sir Thomas Erpingham.

An amusing tale is told by Harrod of Roger Bigod's burial in the cathedral. He was the founder of Thetford Priory, and died in 1107, leaving directions that his body should be buried in his own monastery. The prior of Thetford was much perplexed to hear that Bishop Herbert had taken possession of the body, and had determined that it should be interred with all the due solemnities at Norwich. Herbert was anxious to secure for his own foundation so valuable a source of income as the offerings and celebrations at the tomb of a pious man like Bigod; and no doubt the prior was not actuated alone by love for his departed abbot. The bishop won, and Roger Bigod was buried in the cathedral, possibly in the same crypt which is supposed to contain the bones of Herbert himself.

The North Transept, like the south, is without aisles or triforium, the wall space up to the clerestory level being decorated with wall arcading, varying considerably in position and detail in each compartment. The clerestory follows round from the nave, and overhead is the later lierne vault. It was, together with the eastern arm of the cathedral, closed for two and a half years, during which period the whole of the lime-white and paint encrusting the stonework was flaked off. The work, so far as we can understand, was really a restoration, inasmuch as the original stonework was restored to view. The level of the floor was made to correspond with that of the choir, and a raised wooden floor with the benches thereon removed. The transepts were built by Herbert, the first bishop and founder. Both originally had an apsidal chapel on the eastern wall, but only that on the

THE CHOIR APSE

north arm remains, and access to this now is not possible from the transept. Dedicated at one time to St. Anne, it is now used as a store-house.

The vault was added by Bishop Nykke, and was necessitated by a fire in 1509, which consumed the wooden roofs of both transepts. During the recent works the small arcading immediately under the line of the vault was discovered walled up, the builders of the later vault in all probability having done this, as in many cases the line of the vault cuts over the arcading. This was opened up, and is distinctively interesting in helping to reconstruct the original finish to the Norman work under the roof.

The Tower and Triforium Walks, to which access is gained by a staircase in the east wall of north transept, are of much interest. In the triforium the imposition of the later work on the Norman is clearly noticeable, and the original Norman triple windows walled up with the wall shafts which once supported the semi-arches of the triforium roof. Some of the best views of the interior are to be gained from the triforium and clerestory paths.

Interior of Tower.—A continuation of the same staircase leads to the clerestory, and from thence access is gained to the tower galleries. Above the arches of the crossing there is a vaulted passage in the thickness of the tower walls, with six arches pierced in the inner wall, so that the parts of the interior can be seen from this walk. Above occurs a smaller wall arcade, stopped before reaching the angle to admit of large circular holes being deeply recessed in the walls; and above this again another vaulted gallery, with three windows on either side, pierced through the tower. In the lower of these walks openings occur through the thickness of the walls into the presbytery, the nave, and transepts, just under the vaults, and interestingly quaint peeps can be gained through them.

The **Processional Path**, or aisles to the presbytery, consists of four bays to the north and south, with quadripartite vaulting, with a similar five following round the line of the apse. A door in the north aisle leads out into the gardens of the bishop's palace, and from thence the exterior of this part of the cathedral is best seen.

Crossing the north aisle to the presbytery, at the fourth bay eastward past the tower, marked F on plan, there occurs a curious bridge chapel spanning the aisle, access thereto being gained by a newel staircase on the north side. In our notes on the Presbytery, we have referred to the uses assigned to this structure and its connection with the Easter sepulchre. It formed the ante-chapel to the reliquary chapel projecting northward from the outer wall of the cathedral; it probably was built as a bridge so that relics and symbols might be exhibited thereon to processions passing along underneath. It is decorated in character, and the vault is constructed of chalk. The chapel above is decorated with frescoes, the subjects of which are as follow:—In the western quarter of the four-part vault, The Blessed Virgin between SS. Margaret and Catherine; in the eastern, SS. Andrew, Peter, and Paul; in the northern, SS. Martin, Nicholas, Richard; in the southern, SS. Edmund, Lawrence, and a bishop; a figure of Christ occurs centrally. Copies of these frescoes have been made in facsimile, and hang in the aisle and consistory court. Passing through the small door in the north wall of the north aisle before mentioned to the outside, the lines of the reliquary chapel can be plainly seen, and also of another to the west; the position of both these chapels is shown by dotted lines on the plan.

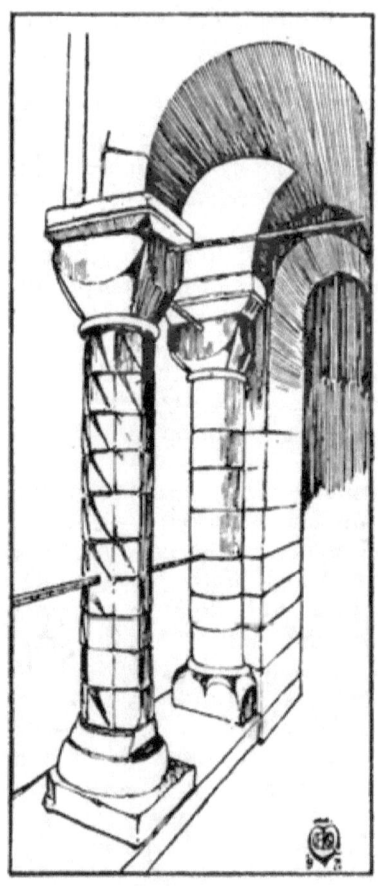

DETAIL OF THE CLERESTORY, NORTH TRANSEPT.
[From a Drawing by the Author.

B. Bolas & Co., Photo.]
THE SOUTH AISLE OF PRESBYTERY, LOOKING EAST.

A coped coffin lid of Purbeck marble, now in the aisle of presbytery, should be noticed; an inscribed brass once occupied the bevelled edge.

The Chapels.—In the Norman cathedral, grouped round the east end of the presbytery, was a trefoil of chapels; the one on the north, the Jesus Chapel, yet remains, and as

Photochrom Co. Ltd., Photo.]
NORMAN WORK IN THE LANTERN OF TOWER.

well its fellow on the south. The Lady Chapel, or easternmost of the three (shown on plan by dotted lines) was succeeded by an Early English building, which, in its turn, was destroyed; the entrance arches, of beautiful proportion, alone remaining.

The Jesus Chapel formerly belonged to the bishop. On plan its shape is that of segments of circles joined, the altar placed in the smaller part. A simple wall arcade runs round the lower half, the whole being covered by a plain quadri-partite vault. The windows are insertions of Perpendicular work, varied in character from the Norman work of the chapel

Photochrom Co. Ltd., Photo.]
THE ANTE-RELIQUARY BRIDGE CHAPEL.

itself. The mural colouring is a restoration; it may be something like the original, but the general effect is somewhat garish.

DOORWAY AND SCREEN BETWEEN SOUTH TRANSEPT AND AISLE OF PRESBYTERY.

THE INTERIOR

The altar consists of a slab of grey Barnack-stone, with Purbeck inlaid, the whole being supported on shafts.

The tomb of Sir Thomas Wyndham, now in the north of nave, at one time stood here, as also the pelican lectern now in the choir.

In Britton, the chapel is shown divided off from the aisle by a stone screen of Perpendicular character; this was removed, and used to form in part the present screens dividing the antechoir from the aisles.

A room over the Jesus Chapel, once the plumbery, is now used as a museum.

The Entrance which led to the Lady Chapel is immediately behind the apse, and takes the form of a double arch with clustered columns to the jambs and central pier; the archivolt is deeply moulded and enriched with the typical Early English "dog-tooth" ornament. In the spandrel over the pier, and between the archivolts, is a quatrefoiled opening fitting just under the line of the semi-circular Norman vault. The arches, walled-in up to the impost level, are now filled with glass, as well as the opening. The original circular Norman Lady Chapel was destroyed in part by the fire of 1169; it was repaired by Bishop De Turbe (1146-74), but it was not until the time of Walter de Suffield (1245-57) that it was decided to pull it down and rebuild a chapel in the style of the period—viz. Early English; it was this later building that Dean Gardiner (1573-89) destroyed.

Dean Goulburn, in his work on the cathedral, points out that it was the *cultus* of the Blessed Virgin, which gathered strength all over Europe during the twelfth and thirteenth centuries, that led to the erection of such sumptuous chapels as this thirteenth-century Lady Chapel of Norwich must have been. When the theological reaction followed, they fell into disuse and neglect, and their final ruin followed when it was found cheaper to pull them down than keep them in repair.

The beautiful proportion of the entrance arches still remaining, the archivolt enriched with the "dog-tooth" moulding—the only example of this particular ornament at Norwich—gives one an idea of what the chapel may have been like. During the recent works of reparation in the choir, pieces of stone were found with the "dog-tooth" built inwards: evidently the stone from the pulled down chapel had been used by the masons for the repair of the fabric.

St. Luke's Chapel, on the south side of the apse corresponding with the Jesus Chapel on the north, was formerly the chapel of the prior. It is now used as the parish church of St. Mary in the Marsh. It has been much restored, and the Decorated windows shown in Britton's view of the east end of the cathedral were replaced early in the sixties, by what the restorer would no doubt have called Norman.

The coloured glass was inserted to the east window in 1868, the south window in 1870, the west window in 1881. That in the east and south is by Hardman, in the west by Clayton & Bell. The glass in the south window forms a memorial to Adam Sedgwick, Professor of Geology at Cambridge, and canon of the cathedral for many years.

The room over the St. Luke's Chapel is used as the **Treasury and Muniment Room.**

The Bauchon Chapel — corrupted to Beauchamp — dedicated to St. Mary-the-Less, projects to the south of the third bay of the presbytery aisle past the tower, (marked B on plan). It was founded in the fourteenth century and the vault added in the fifteenth century. Its bosses represent the Life, Death, and Assumption of the Virgin. The chapel is now used as the consistory court. The bishop's throne, erected by Dean Lloyd late in the eighteenth century in the choir, has found a resting-place here.

A chapel, founded by Bishop Wakering, and which is said to have been used as the chapter-house after the demolition of that structure, came between the Bauchon Chapel and the east wall of the south transept. Its exact position is, however, doubtful. Harrod, quoting Blomfield, speaks of another chapel that was dedicated to St. Osyth, and which was paved in 1398.

The South Transept. — The screen and doorway filling the Norman arch between the south aisle of presbytery and the south transept should be noticed; it is an interesting piece of work of late Perpendicular design. There is a tradition that the Puritans disliked especially any tracery that took the form of this piece of screen work, calling windows in which it occurred "wicked windows." The intersection of the lines of the tracery made the monogram of the Blessed Virgin; and the fanatics destroyed such work wherever noticed. The tale is interesting, though we cannot vouch for its truth.

S. B. Bolas & Co., Photo.]
VIEW ACROSS THE APSE FROM THE CHAPEL OF ST. LUKE.

At the time the whitewash and paint covering the south transept was cleaned off a range of small arcading was discovered immediately under the line of the vault, as in the north transept, walled-up evidently when the vault was added.

The south transept had in Norman times a circular chapel projecting eastward similar to that remaining to the north transept. This was replaced by a later sacristy during the fifteenth century, and the line of this roof can be seen from the outside.

Across the south end there was formerly a stone screen built by Bishop Lyhart (1446-72) communicating with the vestry on the east side, and on the west with the staircase to rooms above the east walk of cloisters. These rooms, as we have before noted, were in all probability the dormitories of the monks, placed that they might so conveniently gain access to the cathedral for the services.

On the top of Lyhart's screen came a clock; there are records in the sacrists' rolls of materials used in the construction of an earlier clock that was made between 1322-25—of two hundred pieces of Caen stone and ten of "Gobetz" used to make a base, and that for making thirty images to represent the days of the month, no less than 47s. 4d. was paid.

The vault was added by Bishop Nykke at the same time as that to the north transept; the carved bosses representing the early history of Christ—the Presentation, Baptism, etc.

The painted glass window on the east side, the subject of which is the Ascension (after Raphael), was erected by the widow of Dean Lloyd about a century since. Speaking of its original position in the triforium of the presbytery, Britton says "it disfigures, rather than ornaments, its station"; it can safely be added that it fulfils the same purpose still.

Monuments.—Chantrey's statue of Bishop Bathhurst (d. 1837), originally in the presbytery, has been placed here in the south transept. The west wall has a memorial to the men and officers of the 9th (East Norfolk) Regiment of Foot who fell in China and Japan.

The east wall has a similar tablet to those of the same regiment who fell in Afghanistan, 1842. A monument, originally on the west wall, to Bishop Scambler (1585-95), has been removed to the south aisle of nave.

The county of Norfolk is peculiarly rich in painted screens

of the fourteenth and fifteenth centuries; and it would have been strange indeed if no specimen of their work had been preserved in the cathedral. Fortunately, a superb **retable** in five panels, representing scenes in the Passion of our Lord was discovered by Professor Willis in 1847, and is now preserved in the aisle outside the Jesus Chapel.

This was formerly an altar-piece to the Jesus Chapel, and was preserved by the happy accident of its admirable carpentry having saved it for the purposes of a table. It appears to have been the work of an Italian artist of about 1370 A.D., and is executed in a kind of *gesso* work. The size is now 7 ft. 5½ ins. × 2 ft. 4 ins.; but it was formerly surrounded by an ornamented frame, of which portions remain on three sides. The subjects represented are—from the left—The Scourging, Bearing the Cross, the Crucifixion, the Resurrection, and the Ascension.*

Traces of other decorative painting have also been discovered in the Sacrist's Room, St. Luke's and the Jesus Chapels, the choir aisles, and other places.

* Royal Arch. Institute: Norwich volume, p. 198.

F. G. M. Beaumont, Photo.]
THE RESURRECTION: FROM THE PAINTED RETABLE
FORMERLY IN THE JESUS CHAPEL.

CHAPTER IV

THE SEES OF THE EAST ANGLIAN BISHOPS

HERBERT, surnamed de Losinga, transferred the see from Thetford to Norwich in 1094, and it is from this period that the history of the cathedral may be said to commence; but, to understand rightly the history of the diocese, we must go back some four centuries and a half to that earlier period when Redwald, king of the East Angles, was first converted to Christianity while paying a visit to the court of Ethelbert in Kent. He, however, proved but a weak disciple, and on being urged by his wife to be true to the old gods, he tried to effect a compromise and worship Jehovah and Baal.

He was succeeded by his son Eorpwald, who was converted by missionaries sent by Edwin king of Northumbria. His reign, however, was short, and at his death the people again relapsed into heathenism.

Christianity was finally established among the East Angles by Sigeberht, Eorpwald's brother, and it was due to him and through his influence that Felix, a missionary from Burgundy, was enabled to fix his see at Dunwich, A.D. 630.

Felix (630-47) must needs have been a man strong in his Faith; he christianised the whole of that district which now includes Norfolk, Suffolk, and Cambridgeshire. He died on the 8th of March, and was canonized after death. Felixstowe, where he is said to have founded schools, keeps his memory green in the East Country; but Dunwich, where he fixed his see, has long since been covered by the encroaching waves.

Sigeberht resigned the crown to his kinsman Egric, and had entered a monastery to finish his days in peace. But the kingdom was invaded by the Mercians under Penda, and the peaceful old king was compelled to appear in the field to give heart and courage to the East Angles. He, however, declined to employ carnal weapons, and went out against his enemies armed with nothing more formidable than a wand. He was killed in the ensuing engagement, and his successor, Egric, shared the same fate.

The administration of the two successors to Felix lasted twenty-two years, from A.D. 647-69. The East Anglian see was then divided by Theodore, Archbishop of Canterbury, into two separate administrations, **Acci**, the fourth successor to Felix, taking Dunwich, while **Beadwin** was consecrated to the see of Elham.

From this date there were two lines of East Anglian Bishops ; ten diocesans followed after Acci at Dunwich, and nine after Beadwin at Elmham.

St. Humbert (828-78) was the last of the Bishops of Elmham ; he crowned St. Edmund king of the East Angles, and both were murdered by the Danes under Hinguar in 870.

After Humbert's death the two sees were again united under **Wildred**, who at this time was Bishop of Dunwich ; he, however, preferred Humbert's see at Elham, and removed there, and so the bishopric of Dunwich became extinct.

During the next two hundred years (870-1070), there were thirteen bishops of Elmham, and then Elmham shared a similar fate to Dunwich, and the see was moved to Thetford by **Herfast**, a chaplain of William the Conqueror. William of Malmesbury records that Herfast had decided to go down to posterity as a man *who had done something*, and fixed on this removal as an easy solution of the difficulty.

William Galsagus (1086-91) or de Beaufeu succeeded Herfast, and he in turn was succeeded by Herbert de Losinga, who became first Bishop of Norwich.

The history of **Herbert's** episcopate (1091-1119) is the history of the causes which effected the building of Norwich Cathedral, and, although given previously in the history of the fabric, must needs be briefly recapitulated here. Herbert, if not of Norman birth, had received his education in Normandy and was Prior of Fécamp—where he had first taken his vows—when offered by William Rufus the appointment of Abbot of Ramsey. The see of Thetford fell vacant, and Herbert procured his own appointment from the Red King in consideration of a sum of £1900 which he paid into the royal treasury. The remorse which followed on this sin of simony compelled him to go to Rome and seek the consolation and forgiveness of Pope Urban. This was in 1094. He returned, and as expiation for his sin founded the Priory of Norwich, the first stone of which was laid in 1096, the see being removed from Thetford in accordance with the decree of Lanfranc's Synod, held in 1075, that all bishops should fix their sees in the principal town in their dioceses.

In cathedral monasteries the bishop, who was elected by the monks, appears to have represented the abbot and took precedence of the prior. Before Herbert's time, the chapter was composed of secular canons and not monks.

Herbert, in 1101, placed sixty monks at Norwich, and it may be of interest to quote from Taylor's "*Index Monasticus*" the establishment of the monastery from Herbert's time up to the dissolution in 1538—

The Bishop representing the Abbot.	Chaplains.
The Lord Prior.	Precentor or chanter.
The Sub-Prior.	Sub-chanter.
60 Monks.	Infirmarer.
Sacrist.	Choristers.
Sub-sacrist.	Keeper of the Shrines.
Cellarer or bursar.	Lay Officers.
Camerarius or chamberlain.	Butlers.
Almoner.	Granarii.
Refectorer.	Hostilarii.
Pittancier.	Carcerarius or gaoler.

Archbishop Anselm had refused to acknowledge that the king had the right to exercise a suzerainty over the Church, and declined to consent to lay investitures. An embassy was sent to Rome, and Herbert, who went there a second time about 1116, represented the king. It, however, was in no way satisfactory; the Pope did not want to offend the king, and he wished to retain to himself the right of investiture, so, while congratulating the Archbishop's representatives, he sympathised also with those of the king. The exertion told on Herbert, and at Placentia, on the return journey, he fell sick, and stopped there until he became sufficiently convalescent to journey by short and easy stages to his own cathedral city. He lived to complete much important business, but his days of administration were drawing to a close. He had been Prior of Fécamp, Abbot of Ramsey, Sewer to William Rufus, had governed the East Anglian bishopric first from the episcopal see at Thetford, had transferred it to Norwich, and founded the Cathedral Priory, and if this were not sufficient, he founded and endowed many other churches and monasteries in the East Country. His repentance had been sincere, and in one of his letters he refers to "my past life, which, alas! is darkened by many foul sins." Dean Goulburn credits him with a third journey to Rome, and says that it was at Placentia, on the outward journey, that he contracted so grievous a sickness that he "lay ten successive days without taking food and without uttering a word"; in fact, never reaching Rome, but waiting for and rejoining his brother ambassadors on their return. This journey was undertaken with the view of adjusting the differences that had arisen between the new Primates, Ralph and Thurston. The embassy was not successful, the Pope declining to commit himself to any but the most general statements.

One of the last public acts of Herbert's life was to attend the funeral of Queen Matilda on May-day, 1118. He died on the 22nd of July 1119 in the twenty-seventh year of his episcopate, and was buried before the high altar of his cathedral church.

Eborard (1121-1145), who succeeded Herbert, a son by second marriage of Roger de Montgomery, first Earl of Arundel, was consecrated in 1121.

During his episcopate Eborard had parted with the towns of Blickling and Cressingham, which pertained to his see, to two of the more powerful barons, in the hope of securing the rest of the episcopal property, and possibly with the idea of regaining possession of the same when the troubled times should have passed.

He was deposed in 1145, and it may possibly be that he had favoured the cause of Maude in the civil wars of the period, and that it was Stephen who compelled him to relinquish his see and spend the rest of his life in exile. He had in 1139 laid the foundation of an abbey at Fontenay, in the south of France, and thither he repaired. He died in 1149.

His successor, **William de Turbe** (1146-1174), was elected to the see, and in the year 1146 was consecrated at Canterbury by Archbishop Theobald.

In 1168, Becket had written to De Turbe from Vezelay, a town on the borders of Burgundy and Nivernois, and ordered him, by the Pope's authority, to publicly excommunicate Hugh Bigot, Earl of Norfolk. He had robbed the Priory of Pentnay, in Norfolk, of some of its possessions. De Turbe obeyed, notwithstanding the fact that the king had sent officers to prohibit him from so doing. An absolution was obtained from the Pope, but the king was so far incensed that De Turbe con-

Photochrom Co. Ltd., Photo.
NORWICH CASTLE.

sidered it advisable to rest in sanctuary at Norwich until the following year, 1169, when he received the royal pardon.

Bishop William de Turbe died 17th January 1174, and was buried in the cathedral choir, on the left side of the founder.

John of Oxford (1175-1200) was consecrated at Lambeth by Richard, Archbishop of Canterbury, December 14, 1175; he was clerk or royal chaplain to the king. He had presided over the council of Clarendon, the constitutions of which defined the king's prerogatives in regard to the Church, and chiefly with regard to the question of trying clerks charged with crimes in the civil courts. He was despatched to Rome on an embassy to the Pope, Alexander III., and on its failure was sent by Henry to the Diet at Wurzburg: the king, not having been supported by Alexander, determined to uphold his opponent, and as well he, in direct opposition to the Pope, made John of Oxford Dean of Salisbury, with the result that the future Bishop of Norwich incurred the penalty of excommunication by Becket from Vezelay, "for having fallen into a damnable heresy in taking a sacrilegious oath to the emperor, for having communicated with the schismatic of Cologne, and for having usurped to himself the deanery of the church of Salisbury."

The dispute was referred to the Pope at Sens, where John of Oxford, with his fellow-ambassador, Gilbert Foliot, Bishop of London, repaired; John of Oxford was rebuked by the Pontiff for his misconduct, but diplomatically managed to effect his end and retain his deanery. Henry had met Becket at Chaumont, through the mediation of the Archbishop of Sens, and, the quarrel being patched up, John of Oxford was sent to escort him to England. He landed, December 1, at Sandwich, in the year 1170, and within the month was murdered at Canterbury.

In 1175, the incursion of William of Scotland was checked, and the king himself taken prisoner by Ranulph de Glanville. John of Oxford and others were commissioned to settle terms of peace; and they executed the treaty of Falaice, afterwards ratified by King Henry at York, by which the Scottish king and his barons were under the necessity of doing homage for their possessions. John of Oxford, who had rendered good service to his sovereign, was rewarded by promotion to the vacant see of Norwich; and during his episcopate sent by the king on an embassy to William, King of Sicily, to convey his majesty's consent to the marriage of his daughter Joan with that monarch.

An important step in the administration of justice was taken during this reign—the king divided the country into six circuits, to which certain prelates and nobles were to be sent at certain times to hear suits and save litigants the trouble of attending the king's court at Westminster. John of Oxford was one of a company of five to whom was given jurisdiction over a portion of the country, from Norwich down to Sussex, and from Buckinghamshire and Bedfordshire eastward to the coast.

On the 9th of July 1189, King Henry died, and was succeeded by his third son, Richard: John of Oxford assisting at the coronation. Richard had no sooner been crowned than he led the crusade to the Holy Land, which had been preparing in Henry's time, and John of Oxford was forced to proceed to the Pope to ask for his absolution of the oath he had taken to follow the Cross, on account of his old age and infirmity. This request being granted, for which he had to pay 10,000 marks, he returned to England.

The last public act of John of Oxford—who was one of the most remarkable men who have held the see of Norwich—was most probably his attendance at the coronation of King John. He died June 2, 1200.

John de Grey (1200-1214) was elected by the monks, and his election being confirmed by King John, he was consecrated by Hubert, Archbishop of Canterbury. It was during his episcopate, and through the quarrel between King John and the Pope, that the power of the latter was at length firmly established—a supremacy that was unquestioned until the sixteenth century.

The metropolitan see of Canterbury fell vacant in 1205; the sub-prior, who was surreptitiously elected by the monks, and unknown to the king, travelled to Rome for the Pope's sanction of his appointment. When the king became aware of this he was enraged, and despatched an embassy upholding his nominee, John de Grey. The Pope pleased neither party, and named Stephen Langton as Hubert's successor. The Pope, Innocent, sent two legates, of whom Pandulph was one, in 1211 to England, and on John declining to recognise the Papal claims, he was deposed, and his crown offered to the French king Philip.

The country had been placed under an interdict, and most of the bishops had left the country. John de Grey remained faithful to the king, and actually invaded France with a small force to attack the invading Philip, but soon was forced to retreat. In the end, John submitted, resigned his crown, which was restored to him, and was compelled to pay to the Church as damages 40,000 marks. John de Grey, who had been sent to Rome to arrange this, died on the return journey at S. Jean d'Angelo, near Poictiers, 18th October 1214.

Pandulph Masca (1222-1226) was consecrated Bishop of Norwich by Honorius, 29th May 1222. He is supposed to have been a member of a noble Pisan family, and in 1211 had been sent by Pope Innocent to humble King John, which he successfully did. He was again employed as Papal Legate during the young King Henry II.'s minority, and died in Italy, 16th September 1226, having played a prominent part as politician and mediator.

Thomas de Blunville (1226-1236), the nephew of Hubert de Burgh, Lord Chief-Justice of England, was consecrated in St. Catherine's Chapel at Westminster by Stephen, Archbishop of Canterbury. He died in 1236, and was succeeded by **Ralph de Norwich**, of whom but little is known; and is even supposed to have died before his consecration.

William de Ralegh was consecrated on the 25th September 1239 at St. Paul's by Edmund Rich, Archbishop of Canterbury. He had been a chaplain of King Henry, and having received the education of a lawyer, from 1224-35 he visited various parts of the kingdom as a justiciary. On the death of Peter de Rupibus he was elected to the see at Winchester by the monks, in direct defiance of the king. The Pope's intervention in the end secured him his see. He died at Tours in 1250.

Walter de Suffield (1245-57) was elected bishop by the monks after Ralegh's translation. He chiefly busied himself in building and beautifying the cathedral, and there is no record that he took any prominent part in politics. He superintended a general inquisition (known as the Norwich taxation) into the value of the Church revenues throughout the whole of England. He died May 18, 1257, during a visit to Colchester.

Simon de Walton (1258-66) was consecrated by Boniface, Archbishop of Canterbury, on March 10, 1258. He held (in 1246) the office of justice-itinerant. Of his administration little is known. He was past seventy when he assumed the charge of the diocese. The barons under De Montfort had beaten the king's army at Lewes, in 1264, and in 1266, from their encampment in the Isle of Ely, attacked and sacked the city. Simon de Walton died January 2, 1266.

Roger de Skerming (1266-78) was elected by the monks, and was consecrated by Geoffrey Rages in St. Paul's Cathedral in April 1266. It was during his episcopate that the disturbance occurred between the monks and citizens over the annual fair held on Trinity Sunday, in Tombland. He died January 2, 1278.

William de Middleton (1278-88) was consecrated at Lambeth by the Archbishop of Canterbury on May 29,

Photochrom Co. Ltd., Photo.]
THE GUILDHALL.

1278, and was enthroned, and the Cathedral re-dedicated after the sacrilege and fire, on Advent Sunday, 1278, when Edward I. and his queen were present. He was appointed a guardian of the realm, 1279, during the king's absence in

France; Archdeacon of Canterbury in 1276; and also steward of Bordeaux. He died September 1, 1288, at Terling, in Essex, and his remains were carried in state to Norwich, and there buried in the Lady Chapel.

Ralph de Walpole (1289-99) was of Norfolk extraction, and an archdeacon of Ely. He was consecrated to the see on Mid-lent Sunday, 1289, at Canterbury, by John Peckham archbishop. His election, however, was displeasing to the diocese. He was translated to Ely in 1299.

John Salmon (1299-1325), prior of Ely, had been elected bishop by the monks, but was appointed to the see at Norwich at the same time that Walpole was translated to Ely. He was consecrated by Archbishop Winchelsey October 3, at Canterbury, and was one of the envoys sent to the Court of Philip the Fair King of France, to arrange the marriage of the young king Edward II. (1307). He was appointed chancellor of the realm in 1320. He also went to France again in 1325; and it was on his return that he died July 6, 1325.

William de Ayerminne (1325-36) was elected to the see by papal bull in 1325, and this overruled the election by the monks of Robert de Baldock. Ayerminne was consecrated to the see September 15, 1325. He had held a prebendal stall at St. Paul's in 1313 and in the next year at Lincoln. In 1324 he was sent as ambassador to Robert Bruce to treat for peace. He died at Charing, March 27, 1336; and was buried in the cathedral before the high altar. He appears to have been cunning and crafty, and not above changing his political views when occasion demanded.

Anthony de Beck (1337-43) was nominated by the Pope, the monks having chosen Thomas de Hemenhale, who however, went to Worcester. Both were consecrated to their respective dioceses by the Pope at Avignon March 30, 1337. He had been Dean of Lincoln. In 1342 he resisted the Archbishop Stratford's visitation; this must have been a foretaste to the monks of his imperious temper. In 1343 he was poisoned by his own servants.

William Bateman (1344-54), of a Norwich family, had been archdeacon of Norwich, chaplain to the Pope, and dean of Lincoln. He was consecrated by the Pope at Avignon, 23rd May 1344. During his episcopate in (Edward III.'s reign)

1349, Norwich was visited by "Black Death"; over 51,000 are supposed to have fallen victims to the dread plague. He founded Trinity Hall at Cambridge, 1350; was sent to Rome on an embassy there. He died January 6, 1354. He was buried at the church of St. Mary of Avignon.

Thomas Percy (1355-69), brother of Henry Percy, Earl of Northumberland, against the wishes of the monks, was elected to the see. He was consecrated January 3, 1355, at Waverly, in Surrey, by the Bishops of Winchester, Sarum, and Chichester. The nobility at this time were securing church preferments for their families to keep pace with the formation of the professions and general advance of learning. He died August 8, 1369, and was buried in the cathedral, before the rood loft.

Henry le Dispencer (1370-1406) was consecrated at Rome, 21st April 1370. He was hated by the monks, who had no share in his election. He was of martial feeling, and took a prominent part in quelling the local disturbance incident on Wat Tyler's rebellion, 1381. He was employed by Urban VI. against his rival, Pope Clement VII.; was arrested for treason in 1399, and pardoned by Henry IV. He died 1406.

Alexander de Totington (1407-13), prior of Norwich, was elected by the monks in September 1406. This election found no favour at the Court, and he was imprisoned at Windsor for nearly a year. He was then released, and consecrated at Gloucester by the Archbishop October 23, 1407. He died April 28, 1413, and was buried in the Lady Chapel.

Richard Courtenay (1412-15) was nominated by Henry V., and consecrated by the Archbishop at Windsor 17th September 1413. He was Chancellor of the University of Oxford in 1407-11-13. He died at Harfleur in 1415, while on attendance to the king during the siege of that town. His body was brought to England, and buried in Westminster Abbey.

John Wakering (1416-25), who was elected by the monks, had become keeper of the privy seal in 1415. He was consecrated at St. Paul's by the Archbishop May 31, 1416. He persecuted the Lollards strongly, and during his episcopate many were burned at the stake. Yet his character apparently was far from being harsh. He died at Thorpe in 1425, and was buried in the presbytery.

Alnwick (1426-36) was confessor to Henry VI., and in 1420 archdeacon of Salisbury. He was appointed by a papal bull, and consecrated August 18, 1426. He was translated by papal bull in 1436 to Lincoln.

Thomas Browne's (1436-45) appointment was contained in the same bull that translated Alnwick. He had been previously Dean of Salisbury in 1431, and Bishop of Rochester in 1435. During his episcopate the citizens again laid the priory under siege over a question of dues due to them, and the liberties of the city were, as a consequence, seized by the king. Browne died in 1445, and was buried in the nave, in the front and to the west side of rood.

Walter Lyhart (1446-72) was nominated by the Pope, and consecrated February 1446, at Lambeth, by the Archbishop Stafford. He had been confessor to Henry VI.'s wife, Margaret of Anjou. He died May 17, 1472.

James Goldwell (1472-99) had been ambassador of Edward IV. at Rome. He was nominated by the Pope, and consecrated at Rome, October 4, 1472. He died February 15, 1499.

Thomas Jane (1499-1500) had been Canon of Windsor and Dean of Chapel Royal in 1497; was consecrated on October 20, 1499. He died in September 1500.

Richard Nykke was consecrated in 1501 He was of infamous character, and no doubt stimulated the zeal of the reformers, who may well have contended that the Church which had such prelates surely needed reformation. He persecuted those opposed to him, and burned many at the stake. He was imprisoned in 1535, for appealing to Rome touching the king's prerogative. He died January 14, 1536.

William Rugg (1536-50) was the last Bishop of Norwich before the dissolution of the monasteries. Wolsey's downfall had occurred in 1529, and in 1536 the smaller monasteries were dissolved, and in 1538 the larger ones shared the same fate, Norwich being among the number, the last prior, **William Castleton**, becoming dean. William Rugg resigned the see in 1550.

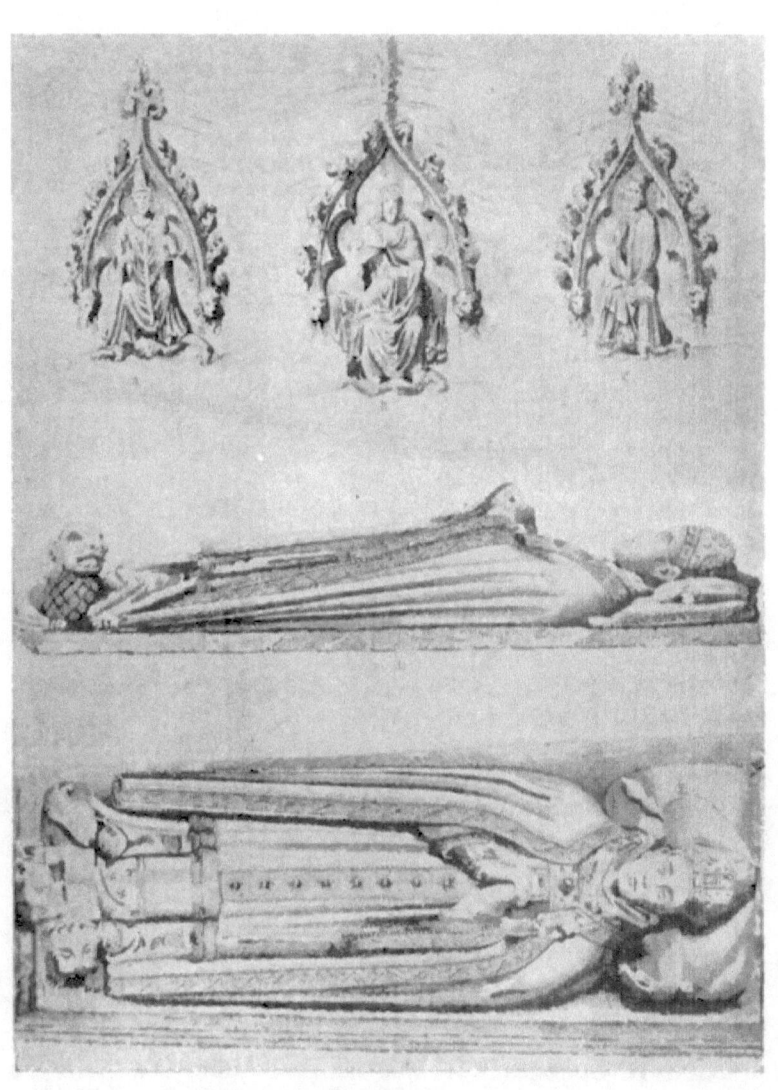

MONUMENT OF BISHOP GOLDWELL.

On the foundation of the cathedral after the Dissolution the establishment was as follows:—

One dean.
Six prebendaries.
Six minor canons.
One deacon reader of the Gospel.
One deacon reader of the Epistle.
Eight lay clerks to be expert in singing.
One organist, eight choristers.
One precentor.
Six poor men or bedesmen.
One sacrist.
Two sub-sacrists.
One beadle of the poor men.
One high steward.
And clerks, porters, auditors, and a coroner.

And such constitution, with but few changes, has held down to this day, the prebendaries have become resident canons, and the precentor is also a minor canon.

Thomas Thirley (1550-54) owed his preferment to Norwich from Westminster to Edward VI. Queen Mary, in September 1554, promoted him to Ely. He was the first and only bishop Westminster has had.

John Hopton (1554-58) was chaplain to Queen Mary, and aided in the persecution of the Protestants.

John Parkhurst (1560-75) is credited with having "beautified and repaired" the bishop's palace.

Edmund Freke (1575-78) was translated from Rochester, and again to Worcester in 1578.

Edmund Scambler (1585-94) was translated to Norwich from Peterborough.

William Redman (1594-1602).

John Jegon (1602-1617) was master of Benedict College for twelve years.

John Overall (1618-19) was translated from Lichfield and Coventry; he enjoyed the reputation of being the "best scholastic divine in the English nation."

Samuel Harsnet (1619-28); translated to York in 1628.

Francis White (1628-31); translated to Ely in 1631.

Richard Corbet (1632) was translated from Oxford. Of him it was said "he was a distinguished wit in an age of wits, and a liberal man amongst a race of intolerant partisans."

Matthew Wren (1635-38); translated to Ely in 1638.

Richard Montague (1638-41); translated from Chichester.

Joseph Hall (1641-56); translated from Exeter. We have quoted in the notes on nave from his "Hard Measure."

THE SEES OF THE EAST ANGLIAN BISHOPS

Edward Reynolds (1661-76).

Antony Sparrow (1676-85); translated from Exeter. He was the author of a "Rationale upon the Book of Common Prayer," 1657.

William Lloyd (1685-91); translated from Llandaff to Peterborough, and from thence to Norwich. He was deposed in 1690 for refusing to take the oath of allegiance to William III.

John Moore (1691-1707); translated to Ely in 1707.

Charles Trimmell (1708-1721); translated to Winchester in 1721.

Thomas Green (1721-23); translated to Ely 1723.

John Lang (1723-27).

William Baker (1727-32); translated from Bangor.

Robert Butts (1733-38); translated to Ely 1738.

Sir Thomas Gooch, Bart. (1738-48); translated from Bristol.

Samuel Lisle (1748-49); translated from St. Asaph.

Thomas Hayter (1749-61); translated to London in 1761.

Philip Yonge (1761-83); translated from Bristol.

Lewis Bagot (1783-90); translated from Bristol.

George Horne (1791-92).

Charles Manners Sutton (1792-1805); translated to Canterbury in 1805.

Henry Bathurst (1805-37).

Edward Stanley (1837-49), father of the late Dean of Westminster.

Samuel Hinds (1849-57).

John Thomas Pelham (1857-93).

J. Sheepshanks (1893).

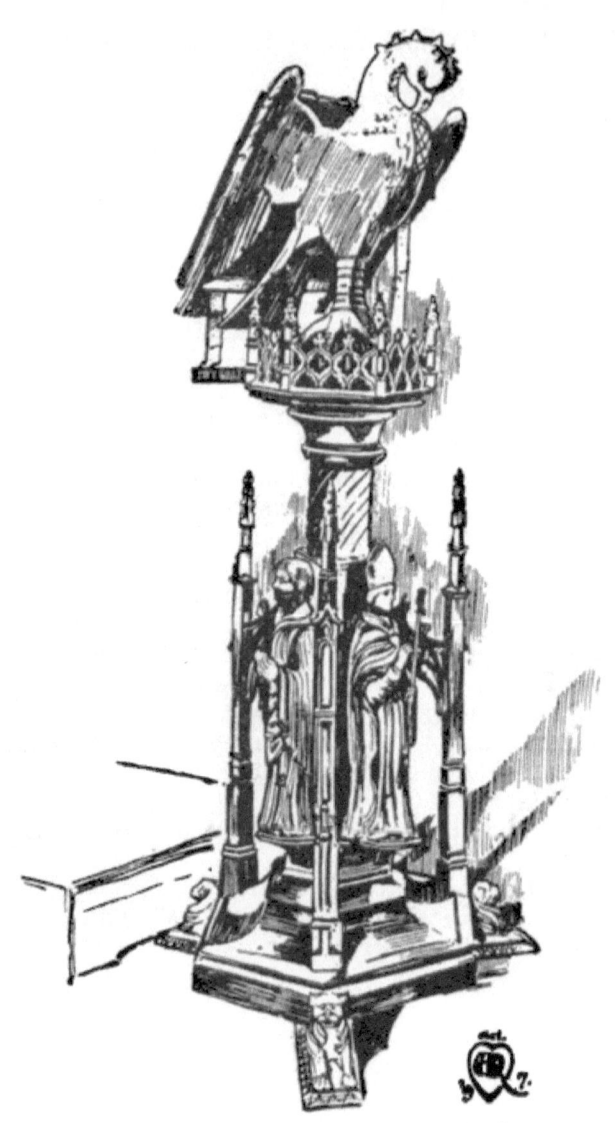

THE PELICAN LECTERN IN THE CHOIR.
[From a Drawing by the Author.

CHAPTER V

THE CITY

THE visitor to this ancient city will by no means wish to confine his attention to the Cathedral and its precincts; but the space at our disposal will not permit more than a list of other monuments which are worthy of attention. Among these the **Castle** naturally comes first. Occupying the site of a very ancient—probably British—stronghold, the first building was erected in early Norman times. For many years it was the principal fortress of the Bigods, Earls of Norfolk, and under them experienced many vicissitudes of fortune at the hands of both Flemings and French. The last event of importance connected with it was the hanging of Kett in 1549. The keep is in dimensions 96 × 92 feet, its height being 72 feet (see p. 99).

The **Guildhall** contains many interesting relics of the civil life of Norwich during the sixteenth and seventeenth centuries, including those of the famous Guild of S. George, established in 1385 and dissolved in 1731 (see p. 103).

St. Andrew's Hall, a fifteenth-century building, was formerly the nave of the Church of the Blackfriars. It contains some good pictures of the English School.

Among the **Churches**, that of St. Peter, Mancroft (fifteenth century), is well worth a visit. Its tower, 98 feet in height, contains one of the most famous peals of bells in England, and has always been the headquarters of a notable band of change-ringers. Of the others, St. Gregory, Pottergate, has some interesting antiquities; St. Giles', St. Helen's, and St. John the Baptist are all of importance: the latter has some good mural painting and monumental brasses, which

THE CITY

should also be examined. St. Michael's, Coslaney, is a well-known type of the Norfolk flint construction.

At **Pull's Ferry** the water-gate to the precincts is still standing. It is an interesting piece of flint work. The ferry itself, of which a view is given here, is a favourite sketching place.

Photochrom Co. Ltd., Photo.

PULL'S FERRY.

THE END

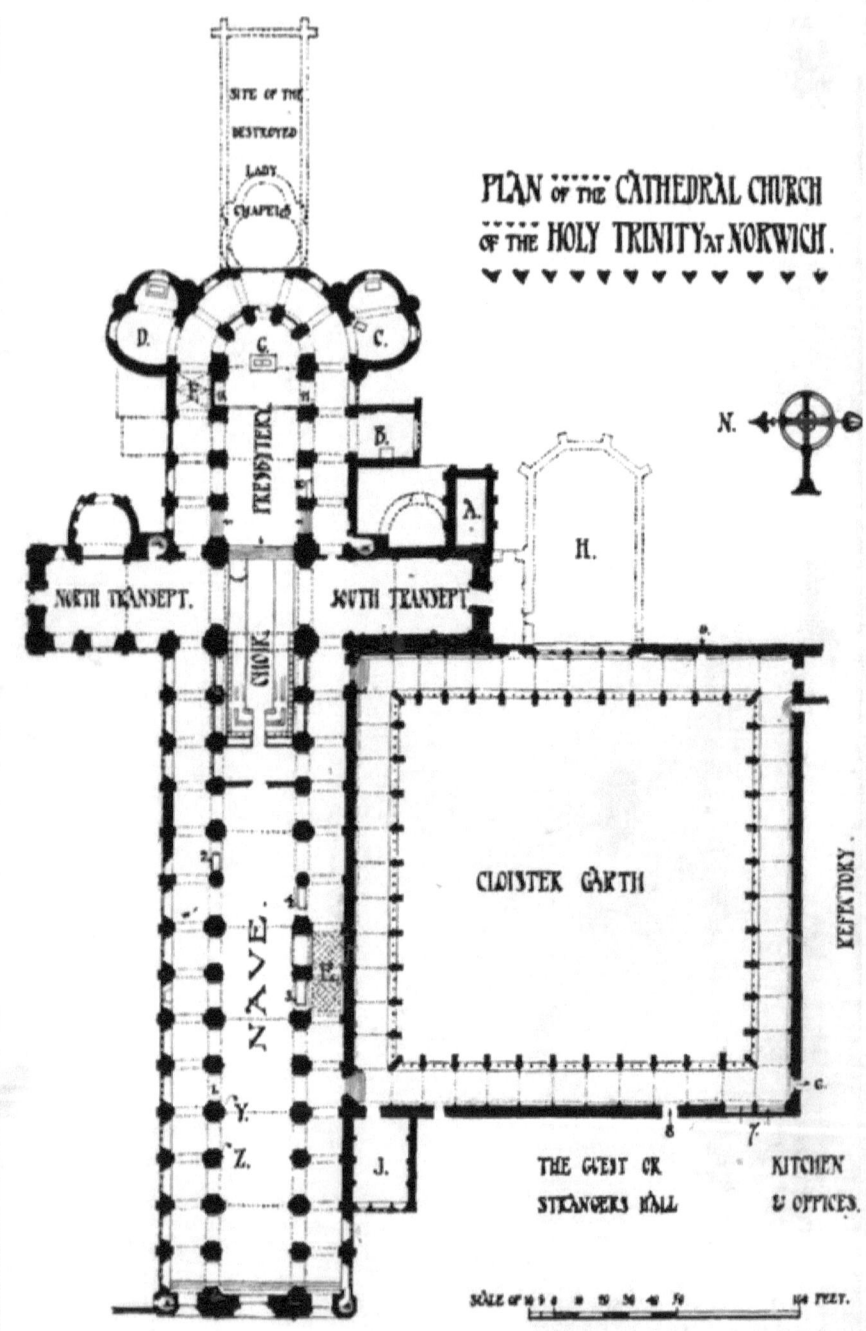

REFERENCES TO PLAN.

A. Dean's Vestry.
B. The Chapel of St. Mary-the-Less.
C. The Chapel of St. Luke.
D. The Jesus Chapel.
E. Bishop Nykke's Chapel.
F. The Ante-Reliquary Chapel.
G. The High Altar.
H. Site of destroyed Chapter-House.
J. The Locutory, now used as the Choir School.
Y. A Main Pier in Nave.
Z. A Subsidiary Pier in Nave.

1. Altar Tomb of Sir Thomas Wyndham.
2.   ,,   ,, Sir John Hobart.
3. Tomb of Chancellor Spencer.
4. Altar Tomb of Bishop Parkhurst (1560-74).
5. Door in the East Walk of Cloisters.
6. Door once leading to Refectory.
7. The Monks' Lavatories.
8. Door once leading to the Guest Hall.
9. The Easter Sepulchre and Burial-place of Sir Thomas Erpingham.
10. Bishop Goldwell's Chantry.
11. The Altar Tomb of Sir William Boleyn of Blickling (d. 1505).

Bell's Cathedral Series.

EDITED BY
GLEESON WHITE AND E. F. STRANGE.

In specially designed cloth cover, crown 8vo, 1s. 6d. each.

Now Ready.

CANTERBURY. By HARTLEY WITHERS. 2nd Edition, revised. 36 Illustrations.
SALISBURY. By GLEESON WHITE. 2nd Edition, revised. 50 Illustrations.
CHESTER. By CHARLES HIATT. 24 Illustrations.
ROCHESTER. By G. H. PALMER, B.A. 38 Illustrations.
OXFORD. By Rev. PERCY DEARMER, M.A. 34 Illustrations.
EXETER. By PERCY ADDLESHAW, B.A. 35 Illustrations.
PETERBOROUGH. By Rev. W. D. SWEETING. 51 Illustrations.
WINCHESTER. By P. W. SERGEANT. 50 Illustrations.
NORWICH. By C. H. B. QUENNELL. 38 Illustrations.
LICHFIELD. By A. B. CLIFTON. 42 Illustrations.
HEREFORD. By A. HUGH FISHER. 34 Illustrations.

Preparing.

LINCOLN. By A. B. KENDRICK, B.A.	SOUTHWELL. By Rev. ARTHUR DIMOCK.
DURHAM. By J. E. BYGATE.	ELY. By T. D. ATKINSON.
WELLS. By Rev. PERCY DEARMER, M.A.	WORCESTER. By E. F. STRANGE.
ST DAVID'S. By PHILIP ROBSON.	YORK. By A. CLUTTON BROCK, B.A.
CHICHESTER. CARLISLE.	BRISTOL. GLOUCESTER.
ST ALBANS. ST PAUL'S.	RIPON.

Uniform with the above Series.

BEVERLEY MINSTER. By CHARLES HIATT. [*Preparing.*

Opinions of the Press.

"For the purpose at which they aim they are admirably done, and there are few visitants to any of our noble shrines who will not enjoy their visit the better for being furnished with one of these delightful books, which can be slipped into the pocket and carried with ease, and is yet distinct and legible. . . . A volume such as that on Canterbury is exactly what we want, and on our next visit we hope to have it with us. It is thoroughly helpful, and the views of the fair city and its noble cathedral are beautiful. Both volumes, moreover, will serve more than a temporary purpose, and are trustworthy as well as delightful."—*Notes and Queries.*

"We have so frequently in these columns urged the want of cheap, well-illustrated, and well-written handbooks to our cathedrals, to take the place of the out-of-date publications of local booksellers, that we are glad to hear that they have been taken in hand by Messrs George Bell and Sons."—*St James's Gazette.*

"Visitors to the cathedral cities of England must often have felt the need of some work dealing with the history and antiquities of the city itself, and the architecture and associations of the cathedral, more portable than the elaborate monographs which have been devoted to some of them, more scholarly and satisfying than the average local guide-book, and more copious than the section devoted to them in the general guide-book of the county or district. Such a legitimate need the 'Cathedral Series' now being issued by Messrs George Bell & Sons, under the editorship of Mr Gleeson White and Mr E. F. Strange, seems well calculated to supply. The volumes are handy in size, moderate in price, well illustrated, and written in a scholarly spirit. The history of cathedral and city is intelligently set forth and accompanied by a descriptive survey of the building in all its detail. The illustrations are copious and well selected, and the series bids fair to become an indispensable companion to the cathedral tourist in England."—*Times*.

"They are nicely produced in good type, on good paper, and contain numerous illustrations, are well written, and very cheap. We should imagine architects and students of architecture will be sure to buy the series as they appear, for they contain in brief much valuable information."—*British Architect*.

"Half the charm of this little book on Canterbury springs from the writer's recognition of the historical association of so majestic a building with the fortunes, destinies, and habits of the English people. . . . One admirable feature of the book is its artistic illustrations. They are both lavish and satisfactory—even when regarded with critical eyes."—*Speaker*.

"Every aspect of Salisbury is passed in swift, picturesque survey in this charming little volume, and the illustrations in this case also heighten perceptibly the romantic appeal of an unconventional but scholarly guide-book."—*Speaker*.

"There is likely to be a large demand for these attractive handbooks."—*Globe*.

"Bell's 'Cathedral Series,' so admirably edited, is more than a description of the various English cathedrals. It will be a valuable historical record, and a work of much service also to the architect. The illustrations are well selected, and in many cases not mere bald architectural drawings but reproductions of exquisite stone fancies, touched in their treatment by fancy and guided by art."—*Star*.

"Each of them contains exactly that amount of information which the intelligent visitor, who is not a specialist, will wish to have. The disposition of the various parts is judiciously proportioned, and the style is very readable. The illustrations supply a further important feature; they are both numerous and good. A series which cannot fail to be welcomed by all who are interested in the ecclesiastical buildings of England."—*Glasgow Herald*.

"Those who, either for purposes of professional study or for a cultured recreation, find it expedient to 'do' the English cathedrals will welcome the beginning of Bell's 'Cathedral Series.' This set of books is an attempt to consult, more closely, and in greater detail than the usual guide-books do, the needs of visitors to the cathedral towns. The series cannot but prove markedly successful. In each book a business-like description is given of the fabric of the church to which the volume relates, and an interesting history of the relative diocese. The books are plentifully illustrated, and are thus made attractive as well as instructive. They cannot but prove welcome to all classes of readers interested either in English Church history or in ecclesiastical architecture."—*Scotsman*.

"A set of little books which may be described as very useful, very pretty, and very cheap . . . . and alike in the letterpress, the illustrations, and the remarkably choice binding, they are ideal guides."—*Liverpool Daily Post*.

"They have nothing in common with the almost invariably wretched local guides save portability, and their only competitors in the quality and quantity of their contents are very expensive and mostly rare works, each of a size that suggests a packing-case rather than a coat-pocket. The 'Cathedral Series' are important compilations concerning history, architecture, and biography, and quite popular enough for such as take any sincere interest in their subjects."—*Sketch*.

LONDON: GEORGE BELL AND SONS.

www.ingramcontent.com/pod-product-compliance
Lightning Source LLC
Chambersburg PA
CBHW020123170426
43199CB00009B/610